DINING IN—HAWAII

Maxine Saltonstall

Foreword by Jim Nabors

Peanut Butter Publishing
Peanut Butter Towers Seattle, Washington 98134

TITLES IN SERIES:

Cover Photography courtesy of Michel's at the Colony Surf
Illustrations by Nancy Walker

Copyright ©1981 by
Peanut Butter Publishing
All rights reserved
Printed in the United States of America
ISBN   0-89716-066-5

CONTENTS

FOREWORD

When I speak about anything in Honolulu I am now talking about my home town. Everyone has always known about our spectacular weather and great aloha spirit but—take my word for it—we also have a selection of restaurants that would compare favorably with the best to be found anywhere.

When my career and I were both young and I was green as guacamole, struggling to be an entertainer in a little coffee house in Santa Monica, my meals were whatever was quick, cheap and available. As my career grew, so did my taste buds develop. Through the opportunities to experience the cuisine of many nationalities in the world's great eating places I have at last come to the enviable situation where I can almost judge a restaurant by the look in the maître d's eye.

I love to eat but I have little time, with my busy schedule, to grope through countless eateries. What a blessing for all you readers—and for me—to now be able to let our taste buds dictate what they will and just by turning a page satisfy gourmet cravings. Or, if your mom is like mine, she might want to follow some of the fabulous recipes, invite the neighbors in and make your favorite dish at home.

Let's see now—tonight should it be Italian, Chinese, French, American, Hawaiian? Decisions, decisions . . . Go-o-o-lly!

Jim Nabors

Jim Nabors

L'Auberge

Dinner for Four

Escargot à la Bourguignonne

Cucumber Bisque

Coq au Vin a l'Auberge

Carrots à l'Auberge

Steamed Rice

Poire Maxim's

Wines:
With Escargot—a dry white wine
With Coq au Vin—Beaujolais or other
light red Burgundy

Marcel and Elvi Baltzer, Proprietors

Marcel and Elvi Baltzer left a promising and relatively secure situation in Paris in 1963 in favor of the Islands. Elvi abandoned a budding screen career; Marcel had been captain at world-famed Maxim's for five years. Upon arrival, Marcel became dining room manager at the Royal Lahaina, followed by similar positions at the Kahala Hilton's Maile Room and the elegant (but now defunct) Arthur's in Waikiki. Then, after nine years in Hawaii, the Baltzers decided to try flying on their own.

Because properties in the Waikiki, Diamond Head and Kahala areas were prohibitively priced, the Baltzers chose Kailua for their restaurant. They considered wisely (and correctly) that if they "built a better mouthtrap" people would frequent their establishment no matter where it was situated. So L'Auberge, the Baltzers' own restaurant/crêperie, became a reality on the windward side of Oahu. To reach L'Auberge from Honolulu is to take one of the most beautiful twenty-five-minute drives in the world, over the scenic Pali Highway to Kailua.

Under the many-talented Elvi's direction, the kitchen at L'Auberge provides ample reason to make this drive—a selection of delectable crêpes, impeccably-prepared Canard à l'Orange, Crab Mornay or Poisson de Madame wait at the end of the road. The Baltzers make daily trips to the market for the freshest produce and choicest meats with which to fill their famous crêpes and other award-winning dishes.

The seating capacity is limited to fifty, so it is advisable to make a reservation. One wouldn't want to have just the beautiful drive to Kailua with no dinner at the end of the rainbow!

117 Hekili Street
Kailua, Oahu

ESCARGOT A LA BOURGUIGNONNE

½ pound softened butter
¼ cup finely chopped parsley
2 large cloves garlic, pressed
4 shallots, finely chopped
1 teaspoon salt
Freshly ground pepper to taste
⅛ teaspoon grated nutmeg
24 escargot shells
24 escargots

1. Preheat oven to 375° to 400°.
2. Thoroughly combine butter, parsley, garlic, shallots, salt, pepper and nutmeg. Put a little of this mixture into each empty shell.
3. Rinse escargots and insert one in each shell. Top off evenly with more butter.
4. Place filled shells on special escargot plates and cook in preheated oven until butter is bubbly, about 8 minutes.

Do not overcook this or the parsley will not retain its fresh green color.

Serve with fresh french bread and a good dry white wine. Any leftover butter may be frozen and reused later.

CUCUMBER BISQUE

2 medium onions, peeled
3 medium cucumbers, peeled
6 tablespoons butter
2 cups chicken broth or water
5 tablespoons flour
2 egg yolks
½ cup heavy cream
Salt and pepper to taste
1 tablespoon chopped parsley

1. Chop onions and 2 of the cucumbers. Sauté with 4 tablespoons butter in a non-stick skillet over medium heat until the onions are transparent.
2. Add broth or water and simmer until vegetables are tender. Strain. Press through a sieve or whirl in blender until smooth.
3. Melt the remaining 2 tablespoons butter in the pan used for vegetables. Stir in flour until well blended, making a roux.
4. Pour in puréed vegetable mixture and stir vigorously until smooth. Cook until thickened, stirring constantly.
5. Beat egg yolks and cream together and stir into hot soup.
6. Reduce heat and simmer 5 minutes.
7. Dice remaining cucumber. Just before serving, stir into soup, season with salt and pepper and garnish with chopped parsley.

Note: May be served hot or chilled.

COQ AU VIN A L'AUBERGE

2 small frying chickens
¼ pound butter
Salt and pepper
½ cup brandy
⅛ teaspoon thyme
1 bay leaf
1 quart red wine
¼ cup milk
12 small onions
4 slices smoked pork, cut in ½" pieces
¼ to ½ cup whipped butter
12 mushroom caps
Parsley

1. Halve chickens and wash.
2. Heat butter in a large skillet over medium-high heat and brown chicken quickly, turning often. Salt and pepper to taste.
3. Add brandy, thyme and bay leaf. Strike a match to mixture and let it blaze, then pour in wine to cover.
4. Let simmer, covered, until tender—12 to 15 minutes.
5. While chicken is cooking, combine the milk with ¼ cup salted water and bring to a boil. Cook the onions 4 to 5 minutes in this mixture. Remove with a slotted spoon or strainer.
6. In a separate pan, sauté the smoked pork in a little butter for 8 to 9 minutes or until browned; drain. Add chicken and onions and simmer 10 minutes more.
7. Remove chicken, onion and pork. Debone chicken; keep warm.
8. Simmer sauce gently to reduce by half.
9. Skim off fat. Blend in whipped butter a little at a time, stirring constantly, until sauce is slightly thickened. Correct seasoning.
10. Sauté mushroom caps 1 minute. Add to sauce, then add chicken, onions and pork. Heat through.
11. Sprinkle with chopped parsley and garnish with sprigs.

CARROTS A L'AUBERGE

1 dozen whole baby carrots
½ teaspoon salt
2 tablespoons butter
1 tablespoon chopped parsley
¼ teaspoon white pepper

1. Wash carrots and trim both ends but do not peel.
2. Put water ¼" deep in a non-stick pan. Add salt and carrots and bring to boil over medium heat. Cover pan loosely.
3. Check for doneness after about 10 minutes. Add more water and cook longer if necessary.
4. When done, drain off remaining water. Add butter, chopped parsley and white pepper.

STEAMED RICE

1 cup long-grain rice
2½ cups water
1 teaspoon salt
¼ teaspoon white pepper

1. Put rice in a colander and rinse under running water until water is clear. Sift rice with hands so every kernel is exposed to water.
2. Bring water to an active boil in a sturdy saucepan. Add rice, salt and pepper. Do not cover. Reduce heat immediately and allow rice to simmer 18 to 20 minutes, or until the water has evaporated.

POIRE MAXIM'S

1 cup sugar
2 cups water
1" vanilla bean
4 pears
Mousse
8 small scoops vanilla ice cream
Sweetened whipped cream

1. Boil the sugar, water and vanilla bean together for 5 minutes.
2. Peel pears, halve them and carefully remove seeds and core.
3. Poach in syrup until cooked through but still firm.
4. Remove from syrup and place on a dry tea towel on a plate.
5. Chill thoroughly.
6. Place in a circle on top of **Mousse**. Fill pear halves with ice cream and decorate with whipped cream.

Note: Canned pear halves may be used—this would eliminate the pre-cooking.

Mousse

4 egg yolks
¾ cup sugar
¼ cup Grand Marnier
1 cup stiffly whipped cream

1. Beat egg yolks and sugar in the upper part of a double boiler, over hot but not boiling water, until mixture is firm and makes a "ribbon" when dropped from the beater.
2. Remove from heat and continue beating until cooled.
3. Add Grand Marnier and fold in whipped cream.
4. Remove to large serving dish.
5. Chill thoroughly in refrigerator.

Dinner for Six

Opakapaka au Meursault

Côte de Veau aux Champignons

Coeur de Manoa, Champagne Dressing

Crème Renversce au Caramel

Wines:

With Opakapaka—Meursault, Goutte d'Or, 1977
With Veal Chops—Pommard, Clos de la Commaraine,
1971
With Crème Renversce—Château d'Yquem, 1967

Hemmeter Investment Co., Owners
Yves Menoret, Chef
Noel Trainor, Manager
Randall Newcomb, Wine Steward

Bagwells is an integral part of the Hyatt Regency Hotel complex in Waikiki. With its three-story-high Niagara-type waterfall in view of the main floor, lush tropical plants and posh boutiques, the Hyatt provides a Cecil B. DeMille setting for this restaurant. Guests are invited to stroll through the dazzling complex and work up an appetite before dining, or to have a sumptuous meal and an after-dinner gawking/walking tour.

There is a studied elegance about Bagwells and an almost sublime quality to the cuisine, but for all that there is no sense of austerity nor of theatrical pomposity. The waiters are eager to please, the maître d' is a model of congeniality, and Chef Yves Menoret is a true master at his craft.

Chef Menoret is remembered by many as the purveyor of culinary delights at Alexis, La Fleur de Lys in San Francisco and the Fairmont Hotel in Dallas—to name a few of his former bailiwicks. To see that the over-all Bagwells production runs smoothly, there is also Siegfried H.M. Brauer, food and beverage manager. Formerly with the Southhampton Beach Hotel in Bermuda, Brauer gained additional experience in France, London and his native Germany before settling at Bagwells.

One payoff for all this experience has been the *Travel/Holiday* Award for four consecutive years. In addition, Chef Menoret recently garnered two firsts in the San Francisco Crab Cooking Olympics, competing with two dozen top professional chefs.

Hyatt Regency Waikiki
2424 Kalakaua Avenue
Honolulu

OPAKAPAKA AU MEURSAULT

Before starting to cook the fish itself, it would be wise to first prepare the **Fish Velouté**. *This would insure a smooth process and eliminate having to keep the delicate filets waiting on a warmer.*

1½ pounds opakapaka (pink snapper) filets,
   ½" thick
Salt and pepper to taste
3 ounces shallots, peeled and cut
½ cup Meursault wine
1 cup **Fish Velouté** (see next page)
¼ pound plus 4 tablespoons butter, cut into
   small cubes

1. Butter an oven-proof baking dish. Place fish in one layer in buttered dish, season with salt and pepper and add shallots and Meursault. Cover and steam over medium-low heat 15 minutes.
2. Transfer fish to heated oven-proof serving dish and keep warm. Keep baking dish over heat and reduce the liquid by half. Stir in **Fish Velouté**.
3. Remove from heat and blend in butter. Pour sauce over fish on oven-proof dish.
4. Brown quickly under broiler. Serve immediately.

Fish Velouté

2 pounds fish bones and trimmings
2 onions, sliced
1 carrot, sliced
1 celery stalk, sliced
3 cups dry white wine
2 bay leaves
1/8 teaspoon thyme
4 tablespoons butter
1/2 cup flour
2 egg yolks
1 cup heavy cream
Salt and pepper

1. Put first seven ingredients in a 3-quart saucepan. Add 1 quart water and bring to boiling point. Simmer gently 25 minutes.
2. Strain stock through a fine sieve into a bowl.
3. Using a non-stick pan, melt the butter over medium heat. Do not let it brown. Blend in flour, preferably with a wooden spoon, making a roux.
4. Stir in the stock and keep stirring until thoroughly blended. Simmer 10 minutes.
5. In a separate bowl, mix together the egg yolks and cream.
6. Add them to the roux, stirring constantly. Bring just to boiling point and remove from heat.
7. Add salt and pepper as desired.

COTE DE VEAU AUX CHAMPIGNONS

6 veal rib chops
Salt and pepper to taste
6 tablespoons flour
1/4 cup oil
1/4 pound butter
1 1/2 pounds mushrooms, washed and sliced
1/2 cup chopped shallots
1/4 cup brandy
1 cup dry white wine
3/4 cup heavy cream
2 tablespoons chopped parsley

1. Lightly sprinkle the veal chops with salt and pepper and dust with flour.
2. Heat the oil and butter over medium heat in a skillet large enough to hold the chops in a single layer. Sauté chops until golden brown, about 15 minutes.
3. Transfer to heated serving dish and keep warm.
4. Sauté mushrooms no more than 2 or 3 minutes in the same skillet.
5. Add the shallots, brandy and wine. Bring to boiling point. Reduce by half over medium heat.
6. Stir in heavy cream and simmer until the sauce is slightly thickened and smooth.
7. Cover the chops with sauce and sprinkle with chopped parsley.

ASPARAGUS AU GRATIN

2 pounds fresh asparagus
¼ pound butter
½ cup flour
2 cups milk
Salt and freshly ground black pepper to taste
Dash of nutmeg
3 egg yolks
¼ pound grated Swiss cheese

1. Select a pan in which the asparagus will be able to lie flat. Add ½" water and bring to a boil.
2. Wash asparagus thoroughly. Place in the boiling water; cover and cook 10 minutes.
3. Melt the butter in a separate saucepan over low heat. Stir in the flour to make a roux. Add milk and simmer 10 minutes, stirring constantly.
4. Preheat broiler.
5. When asparagus is done, drain and remove gently—so as not to break the tender tips—to a casserole dish. Keep warm.
6. When milk-roux mixture has cooked 10 minutes, season with salt, pepper and nutmeg. Remove from heat and blend in egg yolks thoroughly.
7. Pour sauce over asparagus. Sprinkle with cheese and place under broiler only until cheese turns golden brown.

COEUR DE MANOA

3 crisp heads Manoa lettuce
2 egg yolks
1 tablespoon Dijon mustard
½ tablespoon sugar
½ cup apple cider vinegar
Salt and freshly ground pepper as desired
¼ cup olive oil
½ cup salad oil
½ cup good champagne

1. Cut lettuce heads in half. Trim stems and remove outside leaves. Place on individual salad plates.
2. Place egg yolks, mustard, sugar, vinegar, salt and pepper in the bowl of an electric mixer and blend until even.
3. While continuing to blend, gradually pour in oils.
4. Just before serving, beat in champagne. Spoon over hearts of lettuce.

Butter lettuce may be substituted outside of Hawaii but, of course, the texture and flavor cannot be expected to be of the same delicate nature.

CREME RENVERSCE AU CARAMEL

2 cups sugar
½ cup water
4 cups milk
2 tablespoons vanilla extract
4 whole eggs
8 egg yolks

1. Preheat oven to 350°.
2. Boil 1 cup sugar and the water in a nonstick pan or small skillet until caramel is slightly browned.
3. Pour into an 8-cup mold and quickly turn mold about so that entire inside is filmed with caramel. Set aside.
4. In a separate saucepan bring milk and vanilla to boiling point.
5. Beat whole eggs, egg yolks and remaining sugar together. Gradually add milk mixture and stir until well blended.
6. Pour custard into mold. Bake in preheated oven about 40 minutes until set.
7. Remove from oven and allow to cool in mold.
8. Carefully unmold onto a serving dish by first pressing the fingers firmly against the outside rim of the mold and then on the bottom and around the sides. Press serving dish directly over the mold and invert both. The custard should slide out onto the dish.

the Bistro

Dinner for Four

Pâté of Chicken Livers

Bistro Salad

Steak Diane

Chocolate Mousse

Wine:
Bordeaux
or
California Cabernet

Karl Diebold and Michael Pirics, Owners
Raymond Winters, Chef

The Bistro is eminently handsome in decor, seats an intimate fifty-five and has an ample bar, but it's the appealing food and genial atmosphere that keep it at the top. The cuisine is mostly French, though aromatic Italian dishes and steaks maintain an important place on the menu. Co-owners Karl Diebold and Michael Pirics hold that they couldn't remove them if they wanted to—popular demand wouldn't allow it!

Chef Raymond Winters joined the Bistro staff after receiving preliminary cook's training from the United States Navy. Then, twelve years ago, he began preparing original Bistro recipes, guided by entrepreneur Diebold. Now he is a true chef de cuisine in his own right, holding responsibility for the menu in his capable hands.

It was Diebold who created the original Bistro menu. He doesn't say how he came by many of those recipes; he *does* say that his mother early encouraged him to become an electrical engineer. He still feels that being a restaurateur isn't so far removed from that.

As every true bistro should, this one stays open until the wee hours. Late supper may be had from eleven until one-thirty, offering up to temptation such delights as Shrimp Bisque à la Crème, Filet Steak Sandwich with Sauce Béarnaise, Escargots Bourguignons, or maybe a Cherries Jubilee for that sweet tooth.

1647 Kapiolani Boulevard
Honolulu

PATE OF CHICKEN LIVERS

⅛ cup minced onion
1 pound chicken livers
¼ pound butter, melted
⅛ cup brandy
¼ cup sherry
Salt and white pepper, to taste
½ pound butter, frozen

1. Sauté onion and chicken livers in the melted butter for 4 minutes. Do not allow to brown.
2. Warm and flame brandy in a small pan, letting it burn for only a few seconds. Pour over the chicken livers, add sherry and simmer gently for 4 minutes.
3. Put hot mixture in a blender and blend until very smooth. Season to taste.
4. Cut frozen butter into small pieces and add to liver paste. Blend until butter is absorbed.
5. Place in a mold and chill thoroughly in the refrigerator.

STEAK DIANE

Virgin olive oil
8 (¾" thick) petit filets
1 tablespoon chopped shallots
½ ounce brandy
½ ounce Worcestershire sauce
½ cup **Bordelaise Sauce** (see next page)

1. Put only enough olive oil in a skillet to oil the bottom of it. Heat almost to smoking.
2. Sauté filets 1½ minutes on each side for rare, or to taste.
3. Add shallots and immediately splash on the brandy and flame it.
4. Remove steaks to hot serving dish.
5. Stir Worcestershire and **Bordelaise Sauce** into pan, deglazing the drippings. Simmer 30 seconds. Spoon sauce evenly over steaks.

Bordelaise Sauce

1 tablespoon butter
1 tablespoon flour
¾ cup beef stock
¼ cup red wine
⅛ teaspoon thyme
5 drops Kitchen Bouquet

1. Melt butter over medium heat in a small non-stick pan.
2. Blend in flour to make a smooth paste (roux).
3. Add beef stock and wine and stir to form a smooth, shiny sauce of medium thickness.
4. Season with thyme and adjust color with Kitchen Bouquet.

In the restaurant we always have on hand a fresh stock pot, but canned beef broth may be used at home if no stock is available.

BISTRO SALAD

1 head iceberg lettuce, outer leaves removed
1 head romaine lettuce, outer leaves removed
4 to 8 artichoke hearts, halved
4 stalks canned white asparagus
2 hearts of palm, quartered
2 tomatoes, not too ripe
1 Spanish olive (stuffed with pimiento)
Dressing

1. Chill a large salad dish.
2. Break lettuce open and rinse under cold running water. Spin dry in a wire salad basket or shake in a pillow slip with several paper towels.
3. Tear into bite-sized pieces onto chilled salad plate.
4. Arrange artichoke hearts, asparagus and hearts of palm over lettuce symmetrically.
5. Remove tomato hulls. Cut one tomato into 8 wedges and place around rim of dish. Place remaining tomato upside down, slice vertically about ¼" thick and arrange on center of salad like flower petals. Place Spanish olive in center.
6. Drizzle dressing over and serve.

Dressing

¾ cup virgin olive oil
¼ cup red wine vinegar
Scant ¼ teaspoon Colman's mustard (optional)

Mix well. If mustard is to be used, first dissolve in vinegar before adding to oil.

Salt and pepper may be added at table if desired.

CHOCOLATE MOUSSE

½ pound chocolate morsels
1 ounce brewed coffee
8 egg yolks, beaten with wire whisk until
    frothy
1 quart plus ½ cup whipping cream
¼ cup confectioners' sugar

1. Freeze 2 ounces of the chocolate morsels.
2. Combine the remaining 6 ounces chocolate morsels and the coffee in a small pan and heat over low flame till chocolate melts.
3. Add egg yolks and mix well with a wire whisk.
4. In a large bowl, beat the cream and powdered sugar together till whipped. Set aside 1½ cups.
5. Fold chocolate mixture into remainder. Pour into serving dishes and refrigerate for at least ½ hour before serving.
6. Finely chop the frozen morsels. Top each serving with reserved whipped cream and the chopped morsels.

Champeaux's
AT THE TOP OF THE I

Dinner for Four

Crab Meat Calypso

Johann Strauss Salad

Fish Neapolitan

Pineapple Madagascar

Wine:
Chablis Grand Cru, Les Clos

Reiner Greubel, Executive Chef
Horst Futterer, Sous-Chef
Robert Wakida, Maître d'

Superb dining is the hallmark of the award-winning Champeaux's, where dinner is a perfect combination of nouvelle and Continental cuisine and beautiful island surroundings.

Riding the special glass elevator thirty stories above Waikiki to the rooftop dining room is but a preview to the spectacular panorama of mountains and sea. The glittering lights of Honolulu play across the glass walls in ever-changing effect; softly flickering candles cast a warm glow over the meticulously set tables. Impeccable service and unimposing music invite diners to enjoy exceptional food in a leisurely atmosphere.

Executive Chef Reiner Greubel has designed a menu that is varied and imaginative enough to tempt every appetite. The adventurous diner who seeks authentic French cooking can satisfy his taste. The guest who prefers a simple steak or seafood dish will find his favorites, with a sauce or garnish added to make it special. Champeaux's extensive wine list includes many fine domestic wines as well as selections from French, German, Italian, Spanish and Portuguese vineyards.

Ilikai Hotel
1777 Ala Moana Boulevard

CRAB MEAT CALYPSO

1 papaya
Curry Sauce
½ pound crab meat
8 orange sections
1 tablespoon macadamia nuts
4 sprigs parsley for garnish

1. Cut papaya in half and clean out insides, then cut into quarters.
2. Mix **Curry Sauce** with crab meat. Fill papaya quarters with mixture.
3. Garnish with orange sections, macadamia nuts and parsley.

Curry Sauce

1 cup cottage cheese
¼ cup white wine
1 teaspoon curry powder
1 teaspoon mango chutney
10 green peppercorns
1 teaspoon honey
Juice of 1 lemon
Worcestershire sauce to taste
Salt and pepper

Mix all ingredients in a blender and season to taste. Thin with water or skim milk if necessary.

JOHANN STRAUSS SALAD

2 bunches spinach, stems removed
4 to 8 slices bacon, chopped
Salt and pepper to taste
Juice of 1 lemon
6 dashes Worcestershire sauce
¾ cup Italian dressing
¼ cup croutons
6 hard-cooked eggs, chopped
¼ cup grated Parmesan cheese
¼ cup grated Gruyère cheese

1. Wash spinach and pat dry.
2. Cook bacon in a heavy skillet until crisp. Drain on paper towels. Keep warm.
3. Add salt, pepper, lemon juice and Worcestershire sauce to spinach.
4. Toss in bacon crisps and add salad dressing.
5. Sprinkle with croutons, eggs and cheeses.
6. Serve while bacon is still hot.

FISH NEAPOLITAN

2 tablespoons water
1 onion, chopped
3 tablespoons chopped green pepper
1 tablespoon chopped parsley
2 medium tomatoes, diced
½ cup tomato juice
1 tablespoon chopped green or black olives
½ teaspoon salt
½ teaspoon basil
⅛ teaspoon pepper
2 pounds fish filets (opakapaka, red snapper
    or ono)

1. Heat water in a large frypan and cook onion 2 to 3 minutes, or
   until tender.
2. Add remaining ingredients except fish and cook until green pepper
   is soft, about 10 minutes.
3. Add fish, cover and gently simmer about 10 minutes or until fish
   flakes easily with a fork.
4. Remove fish to individual plates. Spoon sauce over and serve
   immediately.

*Be careful not to overcook. Try to serve immediately because the fish
will continue to cook in the hot sauce.*

PARSLIED POTATO BALLS

2 large potatoes
4 tablespoons butter
Paprika
Salt to taste
1 tablespoon chopped parsley

1. Wash and peel potatoes. Using a small melon baller, scoop out as many balls as possible (at least 16).
2. Bring a saucepan of water to boil and cook potato balls 7 minutes. Drain thoroughly and place on paper towels to absorb moisture.
3. Heat butter in a skillet over medium flame, add balls and sprinkle with paprika. Keep balls rolling about so that they are always coated with butter and turn an even golden brown.
4. Test with a fork after 10 minutes. When done, remove from pan and sprinkle with salt and chopped parsley.

ZUCCHINI

2 medium zucchini
Salt

1. Wash zucchini but do not peel.
2. Trim off stem ends and cut diagonally in ¼" thick slices.
3. Steam 3 to 4 minutes. Salt to taste.

I do not advocate butter or any other embellishments for this delicate vegetable—it can stand on its own merit.

PINEAPPLE MADAGASCAR

1 medium-sized ripe pineapple
¼ cup Grand Marnier
1 tablespoon chopped fresh mint
20 green peppercorns, crushed
¼ cup honey
½ cup unflavored low-fat yogurt
12 thin slices papaya
4 sprigs fresh mint
4 strawberries, washed and hulled

1. Peel, core and slice pineapple and cut into bite-size pieces. Marinate in ⅛ cup Grand Marnier, chopped mint and crushed peppercorns. Allow to stand for at least 3 hours in refrigerator.
2. Make a sauce by combining the remaining Grand Marnier, honey and yogurt.
3. Drain the pineapple, reserving 2 teaspoons marinade. Add reserved marinade to yogurt sauce. Divide pineapple into 4 tall glasses.
4. Spoon yogurt sauce over each serving. Garnish with papaya slices, mint sprigs and strawberries.

Columbia Inn

Dinner for Four

Hawaiian Fruit Cup

Ham and Bean Soup

Shrimp Sauté with Fresh Mushrooms

Yakitori

Banana Cream Pie

Fred (Toshi) Kaneshiro, Owner
Frank Kaneshiro, Senior Partner
George Vehara, Chef

Columbia Inn is general headquarters for Hollywood film-industry types, Honolulu's press circles, politicians, sports stars and fans, and for those hoping for a glimpse of such personages. But its greatest asset by far is owner/host Fred "Toshi" Kaneshiro himself—the most avid, loyal Los Angeles Dodgers fan under any sun. Better for your health that Diamond Head should come back to life than to let slip a disparaging remark about the Dodgers in Kaneshiro's presence. But let it be known you share his appreciation and he may let you join him at his home plate table (also known as the Round Table)—the first one on the left as you enter.

The restaurant itself is absolutely without pretention—comfortable and simple—and the menu could be put in the same category. Rather than a formal atmosphere, the air here sparks with action and excitement—of things happening, decisions being made, and plenty of aloha. Just ask any of the locals. They all know Columbia Inn.

A more inconspicuous restaurant opening than Kaneshiro's is tough to imagine. Columbia Inn quietly became reality amid the uproar of the original Pearl Harbor week! It eked through that first day with earnings of seventeen dollars–compared to over $3000 a day by 1975, and more than a million a year entering the eighties. Auspicious stars need not always be bright at first.

Kaneshiro's elder brother Frank is senior partner and guiding hand. Chef George Vehara has been overseeing the kitchen for the past sixteen years. Eugene Kaneshiro, Toshi's son, served two terms as president of Hawaii's Restaurant Association—a wall plaque is prominently displayed, reading "For dedicated service to the Food Service Industries—1977, '78."

845 Kapiolani Boulevard
Honolulu

HAWAIIAN FRUIT CUP

Columbia Inn makes use of fresh fruits in season: kiwi, peaches, mangoes, papayas, bananas, pineapples, melons, seedless grapes, etc. The recipe below is fairly basic and calls for ingredients that are almost universally available. It is up to you to add or substitute locally available fresh fruits.

½ cup sugar
½ cup water
Juice of ¼ lemon
1 (29-ounce) can fruit cocktail
1 orange, peeled and diced
1 apple, cored and diced
½ cup diced pineapple
½ cup diced honeydew melon
½ cup diced cantaloupe

1. Boil sugar and water until sugar is dissolved.
2. Stir in lemon juice.
3. Mix fruits together in a large bowl.
4. Add syrup and mix well. Chill before serving.

HAM AND BEAN SOUP

2 cups small white beans
1 pound ham shank
3 quarts chicken stock
2 teaspoons minced garlic
½ cup chopped onion
⅓ cup chopped carrot
¼ cup chopped celery
1 bay leaf
½ cup salad oil
Salt and pepper to taste

1. Wash beans and soak overnight. Drain.
2. Boil beans and ham shank in chicken stock until tender, about
   3 hours. (Check at 2½ hours.) Add water as liquid evaporates.
3. Sauté garlic, onion, carrot, celery and bay leaf in oil until wilted.
   Add to bean mixture.
4. Continue boiling until beans are falling apart and soup has thickened.
5. Remove ham shank. Dice meat and return to soup.
6. Add seasoning if necessary.

SHRIMP SAUTE WITH FRESH MUSHROOMS

1½ pounds large shrimp
6 tablespoons butter
4 cloves garlic, finely chopped
½ pound fresh mushrooms, washed and sliced
6 tablespoons white wine
Juice of ½ lemon
Salt and pepper to taste
2 tablespoons chopped parsley

1. Shell and devein shrimp under cold running water. Place on paper towels and pat dry.
2. Melt butter in a skillet over medium heat. When the butter sizzles but is not quite brown add garlic, stirring to distribute flavor.
3. Add shrimp. Sauté about 3 minutes, or until shrimp is just pink but not quite done.
4. Add mushrooms and cook for 1½ minutes.
5. Pour in wine and simmer 1 minute.
6. Squeeze in lemon juice and add salt and pepper. Garnish with parsley.

Note: If a thick sauce is desired, make a roux of 2 tablespoons each butter and flour and stir in a little at a time until desired consistency is reached. Do not boil this sauce—only simmer.

Serve with rice pilaf and your favorite vegetable. We suggest broccoli spears, french-cut green beans or asparagus.

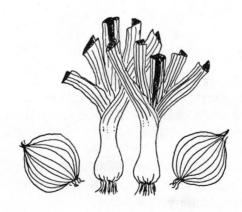

YAKITORI

3 whole chicken breasts or 5 legs, boned and
    cut into 1" pieces
2½ cups **Teriyaki Sauce**
8 scallions, including 3" of green stems, cut in
    1" pieces

1. Marinate chicken pieces in **Teriyaki Sauce** for at least 1 hour in refrigerator.
2. On each of 4 skewers string 4 to 5 pieces chicken meat and alternate with 3 to 4 scallion pieces.
3. Dip in **Teriyaki Sauce** and broil on one side for 2 to 3 minutes.
4. Re-dip and broil on other side 2 minutes.
5. Moisten each skewered chicken piece with a teaspoon or so of the marinade just before serving.

Teriyaki Sauce

1 cup mirin (sweet saki) or ¾ cup pale dry sherry
1 cup all-purpose shoyu (soy) sauce
3 tablespoons granulated sugar
1"-piece fresh ginger root, sliced paper thin
1 cup chicken stock or canned chicken broth

1. Warm mirin in a 1½- or 2-quart saucepan over moderate heat.
2. Take pan off heat and ignite mirin with a match, shaking the pan until the flame dies.
3. Stir in shoyu, sugar, ginger root and stock and bring to boil.
4. Cool to room temperature.

BANANA CREAM PIE

3 cups milk
¾ cup sugar
¼ cup cornstarch
Pinch of salt
2 egg yolks, slightly beaten
4 tablespoons butter or margarine
3 drops vanilla
1 (9") pre-baked **Pie Crust**
2 medium-size bananas
½ pint whipping cream

1. Heat 2 cups milk to scalding in a non-stick saucepan.
2. Add sugar, stir and reheat to scalding.
3. Mix cornstarch thoroughly with remaining milk. Add cold cornstarch mixture to hot milk, stirring constantly with a wire whip until well mixed and thickened. Simmer mixture for 10 minutes, always stirring well from sides of pot.
4. Add salt to egg yolks.
5. Add half of hot milk mixture to egg yolks, stirring to combine. Return egg mixture quickly to pot, stirring until well combined. Mixture must be at simmer when eggs are returned to pot.
6. Turn off heat. Add butter and allow to melt. Bring entire mixture back to simmer.
7. Remove mixture from heat and add vanilla. Stir to combine. Let cool about 10 minutes.
8. Coat pie shell with a layer of custard.
9. Slice bananas into shell, distributing slices evenly.
10. Pour remaining custard over bananas. Chill pie at least 1 hour.
11. Before serving, whip cream to stiff peaks and cover entire pie lavishly.

Note: For a sweeter whipped cream topping, a teaspoon of sugar and 3 drops of vanilla extract may be added to the cream before whipping.

Pie Crust

Our pie shells are supplied to us by a local bakery, but for home use I would suggest this recipe.

1 cup sifted flour
1 tablespoon sugar
½ teaspoon salt
6 tablespoons butter
1 egg yolk
1 tablespoon ice water
1½ tablespoons lemon juice, very cold

1. Preheat oven to 425°.
2. Add sugar and salt to sifted flour and resift into a bowl.
3. Work in butter with a pastry blender until the mixture has the consistency of small peas.
4. Add the egg yolk, water and lemon juice. Gently fold the mixture by hand until the particles adhere and form a ball.
5. Place in refrigerator and cool at least 1 hour.
6. Roll dough out on a lightly floured board to ⅛" thick. Be careful to roll in one direction only—never back and forth.
7. Fill an ungreased 9" pie pan with the rolled dough. Prick the bottom with a fork in three or four places. Trim the edges of any overlapping dough. Press dough around rim of pan with thumb to make a scalloped edge.
8. Bake 12 to 15 minutes, or until golden brown, in preheated oven.

Note: Do not handle dough more than is absolutely necessary, because it tends to toughen it. Also, have all ingredients as cold as possible.

Dinner for Four

Oysters Rockefeller à la Faces

Hot Wilted Spinach Salad

Champagne Sorbet

Opakapaka Meunière à la Pahk

Steamed Broccoli with Lemon-Butter Sauce

Cherries Jubilee

Café Espresso

Wines:

With Oysters—Coteaux Champenois
With Opakapaka—Corton-Charlemagne
With Cherries—Asti Spumanti

Rex's, Inc., Owners
Ivan Philpot, Operations Officer
Peter Pahk, Executive Chef

Bon vivant, gourmet restaurateur, entrepreneur and professional water skier Ivan Philpot is the new operations officer and co-owner of the former Rex's Restaurante. Philpot came up through the ranks of the restaurant business, stockpiling expertise from organizations as diverse as American International Restaurants and the Hyatt Regency Hotel; now he's in a position to put that experience to work for himself and his company.

The restaurant, always a favorite with the young business-executive crowd, draws a steady stream of tourists through word-of-mouth praise. Its central location, comfortably late hours and tasteful atmosphere provide for an after-theatre trade that is often larger than even the dinner rush. Philpot plans no major departures from the established tradition of the place. He intends to continue Faces' already-proven reputation for elegant service and an imaginative, well-prepared menu.

Faces' talented Korean chef, Peter Pahk, favors "a Continental cuisine, very flexible and not limited to what is on the menu." When asked to name his preference for a favorite entrée, Chef Pahk unhesitatingly responded, "a nicely broiled opakapaka [pink snapper] with excellent sauce Hollandaise and a lemon wedge on the side." Indeed, the menu reflects this idea—magnificent foods in a simple presentation—in many of the offerings. Such an idea unites nouvelle cuisine with traditional kitchen practice at its best.

The highest ideals are also maintained in the dining room. All waiters are first apprenticed as busboys to assure consistency of presentation and a familiarity with what might otherwise be some unfamiliar techniques. In addition, all attend a weekly refresher class. Each is thus an expert in the arts of carving and flambé. "Consequently," says Philpot, "they give the best service in town."

3210 Kuhio Avenue
Honolulu

OYSTERS ROCKEFELLER A LA FACES

2 bunches fresh mainland spinach
8 slices bacon, cut into ¼" strips
1 large Maui (or sweet Texas) onion, finely
 diced
¼ cup salad oil
½ cup Pernod
1 pimiento, diced ⅛"
24 fresh bluepoint oysters, shucked, washed
 and on the half shell
¼ cup Hollandaise sauce (see index)
Chopped parsley
Paprika
24 lemon wedges

1. Preheat oven to 475°.
2. Thoroughly wash spinach under cold running water and remove
 stems. Shake out excess water in a wire salad basket or drain on
 paper towels.
3. Finely chop spinach and set aside.
4. Sauté bacon strips and onion in salad oil until bacon is light golden
 brown. Splash in Pernod and simmer gently for 5 minutes, reducing
 slightly.
5. Toss in spinach and cook for 2 minutes.
6. Add pimiento. Set mixture aside and let cool for 30 minutes.
7. Lay a scant teaspoon of spinach mixture in each shell under oyster.
 Also place a little on top of each oyster.
8. Bake 10 minutes in preheated oven (preferably on a bed of rock salt).
9. Glaze each oyster with Hollandaise sauce and garnish with chopped
 parsley, paprika and a lemon wedge.

HOT WILTED SPINACH SALAD

The spinach should be brought out of the refrigerator an hour before preparation so that it can come up to room temperature.

2 bunches fresh spinach
½ pound sliced bacon
2 to 3 ounces Parmesan cheese
4 mushrooms, washed and sliced
2 hard-cooked eggs, grated
2 tablespoons olive oil
3 tablespoons red wine vinegar
Juice of ½ lemon
Worcestershire sauce to taste
Freshly ground pepper to taste

1. Wash spinach carefully under cold running water and pinch off stems. Larger leaves should be torn, not cut, to manageable size.
2. Chop bacon, place in a large frying pan and slowly brown. Stir frequently until bacon is crisp. Strain to separate drippings from bits, reserving bits and, separately, 4 to 6 tablespoons clear bacon fat.
3. Shred Parmesan by hand so as to retain moisture and softness.
4. Place spinach leaves, bacon bits, mushrooms, grated eggs and cheese in a wooden bowl. Toss lightly to mix ingredients before adding dressing.
5. Heat four salad plates.
6. Combine in a french pan (8" oval skillet) over medium-high heat: reserved bacon fat, olive oil, red wine vinegar, lemon juice, Worcestershire sauce and freshly ground pepper. Stir continuously.
7. When dressing is hot pour half over spinach leaves. Return pan to burner. Quickly toss salad ingredients to spread dressing evenly; continue stirring dressing in pan.
8. Dribble remaining dressing over salad, toss and turn onto hot serving plates. Add pepper to taste.

Note: Bacon drippings become unstable and dangerous when brought to heat. Be very careful not to add vinegar late to the drippings, or it will pop and splatter, possibly flaming up.

It is essential that the salad plates be heated before preparing the dressing.

CHAMPAGNE SORBET

¼ pound Häagen-Dazs boysenberry sorbet
3 ounces dry champagne

Fold champagne into sorbet with a wire whisk. Pour into tulip-shaped wine glasses.

OPAKAPAKA MEUNIERE A LA PAHK

Opakapaka is Hawaiian for pink snapper, but red will do.

4 (5-ounce) opakapaka or red snapper filets
2 cups sifted flour
4 eggs, beaten well
½ cup clarified butter
2 ounces white wine
Juice of 2 lemons
6 tablespoons **Garlic Butter**
¼ cup **Bordelaise Sauce**
2½ cups Hollandaise sauce (see index)
Parsley
Paprika
1 lemon, quartered

1. Wash fish under cold running water and pat dry with paper towels. Dust in flour and dip in beaten eggs.
2. Heat butter to an active bubble and sauté fish over medium-high heat, browning both sides. Drain off butter.
3. Add white wine, lemon juice, **Garlic Butter** and **Bordelaise Sauce**. Reduce until you have about 3 ounces of liquid.
4. Remove pan from heat, allow to cool about 30 seconds and remove fish to a warm serving dish.
5. Blend Hollandaise sauce into reduced liquid in pan and spoon it over filets.
6. Garnish with parsley, paprika and lemon quarters and serve.

Garlic Butter

2 tablespoons butter
1 scant teaspoon garlic salt
1 teaspoon finely chopped parsley
Juice of 1 lemon
Pinch of white pepper

Place all ingredients in a small bowl and mix thoroughly.

Bordelaise Sauce

1 can beef broth
2 tablespoons red wine
½ teaspoon minced shallots
Salt and pepper to taste
1 teaspoon cornstarch

1. Simmer the broth over medium heat, reducing by half.
2. Stir in wine, shallots and seasoning.
3. Mix cornstarch with 1 teaspoon water to make a paste and stir into the broth, thickening it just a little.
4. Strain through a fine sieve.

Don't be afraid to "spice up your life." I tend to go for high tang in cooking, to complement basic flavors. Try fresh rosemary with chicken—and be free with the use of oregano and ginger in many other dishes. This doesn't mean to overdo it but you can learn only by practice. The big secret to gourmet cooking is in choosing only the choicest ingredients to start with: the freshest fish, top grade meats— even fresh herbs and spices when possible. Start with that foundation and then exercise your imagination.

STEAMED BROCCOLI WITH LEMON BUTTER SAUCE

1 pound fresh broccoli
Juice of 1 lemon
6 tablespoons melted butter, warm

1. Wash broccoli thoroughly and peel stems.
2. Trim off bottom 2" from stems and score diagonally.
3. Place in the bottom of a wire steamer basket and arrange broccoli tops over.
4. Put basket over cool water in steamer, cover and bring to boil. Steam 5 minutes after water boils for al dente.
5. Mix lemon juice with warm butter. Spoon over hot broccoli and serve immediately.

CHERRIES JUBILEE

A 10" to 12" crêpe pan would be the best vehicle to use. Also, try to have on hand a 6-ounce ladle.

1 orange
8 whole cloves
1 lemon
1 (16-ounce) can dark, sweet, pitted Bing
 cherries
3½ ounces brandy
½ teaspoon cinnamon
2 ounces Kirsch
1½ pints to 1 quart french vanilla ice cream

1. With a sharp knife, carefully peel the orange in a single spiral. Insert cloves into soft side of rind, spacing evenly. Set aside.
2. Heat a crêpe pan over medium flame and grate the lemon rind into it, using about six strokes. Only the outer, yellow part of the rind (zest) should be used. Stir zest around in the pan to extract the oil. This should take no more than 1 minute.
3. Drain cherries and add to pan. Continue to stir as much as possible through the next 2 steps to prevent sticking.
4. Pour in ½ ounce brandy and flame. Sprinkle the cinnamon over flame.
5. Squeeze juice from the orange over the cherries.
6. Stir in Kirsch. Remove pan from fire.
7. Hold one end of orange rind with tines of fork. Pour 3 ounces brandy into ladle and flame it. Hold rind directly over cherries and pour flaming brandy so that it trickles down the full length of the rind into the pan.
8. Serve immediately over individual dishes of ice cream.

CAFE ESPRESSO

At Faces we recommend the use of Cafe Gavina. To brew espresso without the advantage of an espresso machine is simple indeed— although one mustn't expect exactly the same body and flavor.

2 cups water
3 tablespoons good coffee (approximately)

Prepare in a drip coffeemaker and serve in demitasse cups.

JOHN DOMINIS

Dinner for Four

Clams Casino

Dominis Salad with House Dressing

Fresh Island Prawns Alfredo

Stuffed Zucchini

Cassata

Wines:

With Clams—Piesporter Goldtröpfchen

With Prawns—Pouilly-Fuissé

Senator D.G. (Andy) Anderson, Owner
Don Buechner, General Manager
Alfredo Cabacungan, Chef

If you wanted to build an incredibly beautiful restaurant and someone suggested, as the perfect site, a large lot on a dead-end street that was once a city dump—harboring fish auction houses, tuna canneries and the parking area for local garbage trucks—you would probably wonder at the person's sanity. But the owner of John Dominis, Senator D.G. (Andy) Anderson saw beyond the dump and the canneries to emerald waters at the immediate end of the street, waters caressing the lava rock that forms one of the loveliest natural sites in the world for a place in which to dine lavishly.

To quote entrepreneur Anderson, "The restaurant is designed for, the menu is written for, and it's our policy to keep it as much as possible for the local people"—which means that *fish* is the main fare. In the middle of the ocean-view dining room, in a massive six-sided teak wood kiosk, the morning catch is displayed daily on sparkling beds of crushed ice: mahimahi, opakapaka, marlin, ono, aku, ama ama, ahi and mullet. There are also oysters, crabs, prawns, lobsters, clams and every other conceivable Hawaiian-waters catch, including whole fish that are three to four feet in length.

On John Dominis' grounds are lavish waterfalls and miniature reefs alive with spiny lobsters and reef fish. The restaurant also affords a magnificent view of Kewalo Basin in which sailboats, fishing fleet trawlers and dinner-cruise catamarans sail about. The sunset is always marvelous and frequently accompanied by a double rainbow. As the evening lights of Waikiki and Diamond Head replace the diminishing rays of the sun, the view changes dramatically. Lights along the Honolulu shoreline, with no smog or pollution to dim their evening brightness, wink and glisten.

John Dominis is a restaurant of consummate beauty. It also boasts a chef who not only "knows his onions" but has proved himself as well with fish, steak and just about everything else.

43 Ahui Street
Honolulu

CLAMS CASINO

6 slices bacon, quartered
¼ teaspoon anchovy paste
4 tablespoons cream cheese
24 cherrystone clams
¼ cup pimientos, finely diced
¼ cup green pepper, finely diced

1. Preheat oven to 375°.
2. Fry bacon lightly over low heat. Do not let it cook crisp because it completes cooking in the oven later on.
3. Blend anchovy paste into cream cheese.
4. Shuck clams and remove from shells. Save shells.
5. Place a half shell for each clam on a foil-covered cookie sheet. Add 1 teaspoon cream cheese/anchovy mixture to each half shell.
6. Replace clam meat in shells. Put a pinch each of diced green pepper and pimiento over each.
7. Top each with a quarter-slice of bacon and bake in preheated oven only until bacon is crisp, 5 to 7 minutes.

A serving suggestion: If you have any leftover mashed potatoes or rice, place about ½ teaspoon under each clam shell on the serving dish and it will keep them from sliding.

DOMINIS SALAD WITH HOUSE DRESSING

1 head romaine lettuce
1 beefsteak tomato, sliced
1 avocado, peeled and sliced
1 Maui onion or sweet yellow Texas onion,
    sliced
4 anchovy filets, halved
House Dressing

1. Separate lettuce leaves and wash under cold running water. Gently
   pat dry with paper towels or spin in a wire salad basket.
2. Using mainly the tender inner leaves, break lettuce just once or twice
   into an ample salad bowl.
3. Scatter sliced ingredients over lettuce in bowl. Add anchovies.
4. Drip dressing over top. It is not necessary to toss.

House Dressing

1 cup vegetable oil
5 tablespoons red wine vinegar
Juice of ¼ lemon
¼ of a beaten egg
1 tablespoon capers
1 teaspoon chopped chives
1 tablespoon chopped onion
Salt and pepper to taste

1. Combine oil, vinegar, lemon juice and egg in a blender. Blend
   well.
2. Pour into a bowl or bottle and thoroughly mix in remaining
   ingredients.

FRESH ISLAND PRAWNS ALFREDO

24 prawns
¼ cup peanut oil
3 tablespoons minced garlic
1 tablespoon salt
¼ cup cider vinegar
12 ounces beer

1. Remove pincers, antennae and legs from prawns but leave the shells and heads on.
2. Heat the oil in a wok or non-stick pan over a high heat until almost smoking. Add salt, then prawns and garlic. Stir-fry until shells turn pink, then immediately add vinegar and beer.
3. Simmer for just 5 minutes. Be careful not to overcook.
4. Remove shrimp and reduce sauce until syrupy. Serve as a dip for shrimp.

STUFFED ZUCCHINI

2 large zucchini
¼ cup butter
1 cup sliced onions
1 tablespoon chopped shallots
¼ pound fresh mushrooms, chopped
Salt to taste
¼ teaspoon white pepper
¼ teaspoon Aromat seasoning
½ cup dry white wine
1 ounce Swiss or Jack cheese, grated
1 ounce Parmesan cheese, grated

1. Preheat oven to 450°.
2. Wash and trim stems off zucchini. Split lengthwise. Scoop out pulp and chop finely. Reserve shells.
3. Heat 4 tablespoons butter in a non-stick pan or skillet over medium heat. When it bubbles but is not yet brown, add zucchini pulp, onions, shallots and mushrooms. Toss with a wooden spoon until contents are well coated with butter.
4. Add salt, pepper and Aromat. Splash wine in and let mixture simmer only long enough to reduce—5 to 7 minutes.
5. Transfer contents to a collander to drain excess moisture.
6. Brush hollowed zucchini hulls with remaining butter. Shake just a bit of salt and pepper over. Fill each with a portion of the drained mixture.
7. Top with grated cheeses.
8. Butter an oven-proof baking dish and very gently distribute zucchini shells in bottom. Cover dish and bake 15 minutes in preheated oven.

This is one of our most popular and called-for dishes and we feel you will want to repeat the joy of cooking and serving it many times. Don't hesitate to take your baking dish to the table and serve directly from it.

CASSATA

1 (1-pound) pound cake
1 pound ricotta cheese
1 ounce Strega or Grand Marnier liqueur
2 cups confectioners' sugar
¼ pound chocolate chips
½ pound candied fruits
1 cup **Chocolate Frosting**

1. Slice pound cake into 2 layers.
2. Blend ricotta, liqueur and sugar together.
3. Fold in cholocate chips and candied fruits.
4. Spread mixture between cake layers. Replace top layer.
5. Cover with chocolate frosting.

For special occasions the top could be decorated with butter cream squeezed through a pastry tube or applied with a small rubber spatula.

Chocolate Frosting

1½ squares unsweetened chocolate
4 tablespoons butter, softened
2 cups powdered sugar
1 teaspoon vanilla
2 tablespoons heavy cream
2 unbeaten egg yolks (optional)

1. Melt the chocolate in top of double boiler.
2. In a separate pan, cream together the butter and half the sugar.
3. Blend in melted chocolate and the remaining sugar.
4. Add vanilla, cream and egg yolks (optional). Mix thoroughly.

Kapalua Bay Hotel

Dinner for Four

Baked Papaya Walter

Shrimp Obregon à l'Absinthe

Spoom

Wahoo Baloise

Manoa Lettuce with Lemon Dressing

Fried Ice Cream

Wines:

*With the Meal—Blanc Fumé de Pouilly, Wildman
et Fils, 1978
With Dessert, Freemark Abbey Edelwein Gold, 1976*

*Rob Shelton, Dining Room Manager
Hans-Peter Hager, Executive Chef
Jean-Pierre Dosse, Food and Beverage Manager
Jerry Gallego, Dave Wilkes and Eric Birkholm,
Maîtres d'
Jeff Patterson and Eric Hansen, Wine Stewards*

One might imagine that the Kapalua Bay Hotel initiated the idea of nouvelle cuisine—it is exercised with such dedication and stunning success by Executive Chef Hans-Peter Hager. His Fresh Maui Island Sweet Water Crayfish Provençale is truly inspired. Baked Papaya Walter, Shrimp Obregon à la Absinthe and Wahoo Baloise are no less creative, though their ingredients may be more readily available.

Chef Hager studied in Germany, Switzerland and Greece. He worked at the Mauna Kea Hotel on the island of Hawaii in 1965 and then continued on to the Bahamas, New York, Colorado Springs and the Virgin Islands before settling on Maui at the Kapalua Bay Hotel in 1978.

Food and beverage manager Jean-Pierre Dosse's background is equally extensive. There were periods of study in Lyon, Geneva, Lucerne, Zurich, the Isle of Bandor in France, Palm Beach and Washington, D.C., to name but a few, before coming to his present position on Maui.

The Kapalua Bay Hotel offers a variety of dining sites. There is a lavish indoor luncheon buffet, an informal plantation-style veranda for light meals and an enormous open-air dining "room" which seats 205 guests. Dancing is featured evenings from 6:00 to 9:30.

1 Bay Drive
Kapalua, Maui

BAKED PAPAYA WALTER

1½ cups cottage cheese
1½ cups cream cheese
1 teaspoon curry powder
2 tablespoons chopped chutney
½ cup water chestnuts, very thinly sliced
2 tablespoons white sultana raisins
2 papayas, cut in half and seeded
2 tablespoons cinnamon
2 tablespoons sugar
¼ cup melted butter

1. Preheat oven to 450°.
2. Blend together cottage cheese, cream cheese, curry powder and chutney.
3. When well blended and smooth, add water chestnuts and raisins.
4. Fill papayas with mixture.
5. Mix cinnamon and sugar together and sprinkle over papayas. Dribble melted butter over and bake in preheated oven approximately 15 minutes.

If the papayas are extra large, make a little more filling.

SHRIMP OBREGON A L'ABSINTHE

Don't overcook the shrimp—have the courage to remove them from the skillet while still a little underdone. They will finish cooking off the heat and when returned to the boiling sauce.

2 tablespoons butter
1 pound raw shrimp, cleaned and deveined
2 cloves garlic, peeled
Zest of 2 lemons
Salt and pepper to taste
1½ cups heavy cream
½ lemon
1 ounce Pernod

1. Heat butter in a 14" skillet on high heat until butter bubbles.
2. Add shrimp, garlic, lemon zest, salt and pepper. Cook 3 to 5 minutes until slightly underdone. Remove the shrimp from skillet with a slotted spoon and set aside.
3. Reduce the pan liquid until approximately only 3 to 4 tablespoons remain.
4. Add cream, keep simmering and reduce to a medium-light consistency.
5. Squeeze lemon juice into the pan, correct the seasoning, return the shrimp and add Pernod.
6. Bring to boil and serve.

Zest is the colored outermost layer of rind. Using a potato peeler very lightly will easily remove the zest.

This delightful dish will please everyone if served with fresh egg noodles or rice. However, if shrimp are to be served as hors d'oeuvres, fresh toastlets will do nicely.

SPOOM

The internationally acclaimed Walter Blum, executive chef of the hotel's former parent corporation, perfected this version of the traditional palate-freshener.

½ cup water
1 cup sugar
2 egg whites at room temperature
1 pint lemon sherbet, slightly softened
1 cup rosé, white wine or champagne

1. In a medium saucepan over medium heat, boil water and sugar until temperature reaches 238° F. on a candy thermometer or until syrup forms thin threads when dropped from a spoon onto waxed paper.
2. Beat egg whites in a large bowl with mixer at high speed until soft peaks form.
3. Dribble hot syrup in a thin thread into egg whites while continuing to beat.
4. Stir in softened lemon sherbet.
5. Spoon into 4 freezer-proof stemmed glasses or dessert dishes to about three-quarters full.
6. Cover and freeze.
7. When serving, pour approximately ¼ cup wine or champagne over each portion.

Prepare early in the day or up to one week before needed.

WAHOO BALOISE

4 (10-ounce) slices boneless filet of fresh wahoo
3 medium-sized Bermuda onions, peeled and sliced very
    thin
½ cup cream
1 egg
1 cup flour
½ pound butter
1 tablespoon Worcestershire sauce
3 lemons
1 tablespoon chopped parsley
Salt and pepper to taste
Wesson or corn oil for deep-frying

1. Using a deep-fryer, heat oil to 325°.
2. Pre-fry sliced onions slowly, in order to dry onions before they get too much color. If fried too fast, they will get brown and soggy. Remove onions when crisp. Dry on paper towels.
3. Beat egg with a fork. Blend in cream.
4. Dip fish slices into egg mixture, dust with flour and season with salt and pepper.
5. Preheat half the butter in a large frying pan over medium-high heat.
6. When butter bubbles merrily, lay fish in pan and cook evenly on both sides until done—about 2 minutes per side.
7. Transfer fish onto a warmed platter. Sprinkle Worcestershire sauce and lemon juice over each slice.
8. Add remaining butter to frying pan; stir and brown. Butter is ready when it stops foaming.
9. Put all the onions in this hot brown butter and immediately pour the full contents of frying pan over the fish.
10. Garnish with chopped parsley and lemon wedges and serve.

Salmon is also excellent in place of the wahoo. It is prepared this way in Switzerland.

RICE

1 cup long grain rice
1½ cups water
1 teaspoon salt

1. Put rice in a strainer and run tap water over it until thoroughly washed.
2. Measure cold water into a saucepan. Add salt and washed rice and bring to a rolling boil over medium heat.
3. Immediately cover with a tight lid and reduce heat to as low as possible. (If using an electric stove it would be wise to place an asbestos pad under pan.)
4. After 25 minutes, remove the lid and test for doneness.

BUTTERED SPINACH

3 bunches spinach
4 tablespoons softened butter
1 lemon, quartered
Salt to taste

1. Under cold running water, wash each leaf separately and remove tough stems. Discard any brown leaves. Keep in cold water until just before time to cook.
2. Cover just the bottom of a pan with water and bring to boil over medium heat. Add spinach leaves, allowing any water that is clinging to them to remain.
3. After a few moments, toss the spinach in the pan (with kitchen tongs) in order to cook evenly. Wait a minute or so and toss again. Add salt. When spinach is wilted but still fresh-looking, but in no case after more than 5 minutes, remove from heat and drain well. Spoon 1 tablespoon butter over each portion and garnish with a lemon wedge.

MANOA LETTUCE WITH LEMON DRESSING

2 heads Manoa lettuce
1 tablespoon lemon juice
1 cup olive oil
$\frac{1}{3}$ teaspoon sesame oil
2 teaspoons sugar
Salt and pepper to taste
Pinch of Accent

1. Cut lettuce in halves or quarters, depending on size; leave cores in.
2. Whisk remaining ingredients well. Divide lettuce into portions and pour dressing over.

FRIED ICE CREAM

4 (¼" thick) slices sponge cake or white bread, crust
   removed
1⅓ cups vanilla ice cream
2 eggs
¼ teaspoon vanilla
1 tablespoon sugar
¼ teaspoon cornstarch
10 ounces whole raspberries

1. Lay a clean cloth on the table top, then place 1 slice of cake in the center.
2. Set 1 scoop ice cream on top of cake.
3. Raise cloth off table by its corners. Grasp the ice cream through the cloth with one hand, molding the cake around it. Twist the cloth to shape top of ice cream ball and cake into round, but not too tight.
4. Remove from cloth, wrap in aluminum foil and place in freezer. Repeat procedure for remaining 3 scoops of ice cream. Freeze at least 2 hours.
5. Preheat deep-fryer to 375°.
6. Beat eggs, vanilla, sugar and cornstarch in a bowl. When ice cream balls are sufficiently frozen, remove from foil and dip into batter. Deep-fry to a golden brown color, approximately 1½ to 2 minutes.
7. Set on a dry cloth to absorb excess oil.
8. Serve on chilled dessert plates. Top with raspberries.

MAILE
RESTAURANT

Dinner for Four

Shrimp in Snail Butter and Sauterne Sauce

Spinach Salad

Roast Duckling Waialae

Wild Rice and Mushrooms

Frosted Macadamia Nut Soufflé

Wine:
Côte de Beaune

Kahala Hilton Hotel, Owner
Martin Wyss, Executive Chef
Charlene Goodness, Maître d'
Kurt Lapeiner, Food and Beverage Manager

Maile foliage, when made into lightly fragrant leis, are customarily worn at special festive occasions and are a traditional "must" to adorn the bridegroom at his wedding. Certainly the Maile Restaurant at the Kahala Hilton Hotel is acknowledged as one of the most festive dining rooms in Hawaii. It has hosted more wedding parties and graduation celebrants than almost any other place in town.

Maile does not depend upon a panoramic view to make dining attractive —indeed, it is located below the hotel lobby, with no outside view at all. Still, the restaurant itself, with its impeccable appointments and its superb cuisine, has not only expanded its prestige over the years but has almost become a sine qua non for its sumptuous Sunday night buffet.

Executive Chef Martin Wyss, born and trained in Switzerland, joined the staff at the hotel's inception in 1964. He since has brought to the Maile ten *Holiday* Awards.

For reservations one must call Charlie—that is, Charlene Goodness, a Kahala Hilton alumnus since 1968. Ten years as manager of the Maile Restaurant has added only more joie de vivre to this lively young lady, who will arrange anything for you—from a party of forty to a very selective corner à deux.

5000 Kahala Avenue
Honolulu

SHRIMP IN SNAIL BUTTER AND SAUTERNE SAUCE

12 shrimp, 6 to 8-count
½ cup olive oil
Juice of 1 lemon
1 teaspoon Worcestershire sauce
1 clove garlic, chopped fine
3 sprigs parsley plus 1 teaspoon
    chopped parsley
Salt and pepper
¼ cup flour
2 tablespoons butter
1 cup **Snail Butter**
¼ cup sauterne

1. Place shrimp in olive oil, lemon juice, Worcestershire sauce, garlic, parsley sprigs and salt and pepper to taste. Marinate overnight in refrigerator.
2. Dip shrimp in flour to coat lightly.
3. Heat butter in a non-stick skillet over medium-high heat.
4. Sauté shrimp 5 to 8 minutes or until almost done.
5. Add **Snail Butter** and sauterne.
6. Sauté 2 more minutes and sprinkle chopped parsley over. Serve immediately.

Snail Butter

½ pound butter, softened
1 teaspoon finely chopped parsley
½ clove garlic, finely chopped
½ clove shallot, finely chopped
2 teaspoons white wine
¼ teaspoon chicken bouillon base
¼ teaspoon Worcestershire sauce
Juice of ½ lemon
Salt and pepper to taste

With a wire whisk, whip all ingredients together until light and creamy.

SPINACH SALAD

2 slices bacon
2 bunches Horenso spinach
1 cup olive oil
½ cup fresh lemon juice
Salt and pepper to taste
1 hard-cooked egg white, chopped

1. Fry bacon crisp, drain on paper towels and crumble.
2. Trim off spinach stems while washing leaves individually under cold running water. Drain on paper towels.
3. In a salad bowl, mix olive oil, lemon juice, salt and pepper.
4. Put spinach leaves and bacon bits in a bowl. Add dressing and toss lightly.
5. Sprinkle with chopped egg white.

In Hawaii, mainland spinach is known as Horenso. The spinach grown in Hawaii is very good for cooking but, because of the difference in texture and taste, does not do well in a fresh spinach salad.

ROAST DUCKLING WAIALAE

2 (4-pound) ducklings
Salt and pepper
¼ cup granulated sugar
2½ tablespoons water
½ cup red wine vinegar
2 oranges
¾ cup red wine
2 cups **Brown Sauce** (see next page)
1 cup water
2 drops Tabasco sauce
¼ teaspoon Kitchen Bouquet (optional)
16 lichee fruit
12 sections tangerine
16 slices banana
1 ounce Grand Marnier
1 ounce brandy

1. Preheat oven to 350°.
2. Rub ducklings with salt and pepper. Roast 1 to 1½ hours, or until done.
3. While duck is cooking, caramelize sugar in water in a non-stick saucepan.
4. Add wine vinegar and simmer for 2 minutes.
5. Heat **Brown Sauce** separately.
6. Wash oranges and peel with a julienne scraper. In a separate pan, boil julienne strips in red wine for 5 minutes. Set aside.
7. Squeeze juice from oranges into caramel sauce. Add heated **Brown Sauce** and simmer 15 minutes. Set pan aside.
8. When ducklings are done, remove from pan and discard fat. Deglaze pan with 1 cup water and add stock sauce. Simmer 5 minutes. Strain sauce.
9. Add orange peel, wine mixture and Tabasco sauce. If the sauce is not dark enough add Kitchen Bouquet for color.
10. Carve each duckling into four pieces and arrange in a flat skillet. Sprinkle with lichee, tangerines and banana slices. Warm over medium heat. Flame with Grand Marnier and brandy.
11. Spoon some of the sauce over ducklings and serve.

May be served with buttered wild rice and spiced peaches.

Brown Sauce

2 tablespoons butter
2 tablespoons flour
¼ teaspoon paprika
2 cups Swanson's canned beef broth
3 drops Maggi sauce

1. Melt butter in a saucepan and add flour to make a smooth roux. Add paprika. Allow roux to cook until lightly browned, stirring constantly.
2. Gradually blend in beef broth until mixture is completely smooth.
3. Add Maggi sauce.

This is a convenient and simple way of preparing brown sauce for the home.

WILD RICE AND MUSHROOMS

1 cup wild rice
3 cups water
1 teaspoon salt
Mushrooms

1. Thoroughly wash rice in a sieve under cool water.
2. Place water, salt and rice in a covered non-stick pan over medium heat.
3. When water comes to a boil, lower heat, remove cover and cook 30 minutes or until tender. Do not stir.
4. Drain off any remaining liquid, place an asbestos pad under pan over very low heat and let rice sit for about 15 minutes.
5. Add Mushrooms, stirring in gently with a fork.

Mushrooms

½ pound fresh mushrooms
2 tablespoons finely chopped shallots
2 tablespoons finely chopped parsley
¼ teaspoon paprika
Salt and white pepper to taste

1. Rinse mushrooms and brush with a vegetable brush.
2. Slice each cap into quarters and stems into halves.
3. Warm butter in a skillet or saucepan over medium heat. Add shallots and parsley.
4. After 1 minute add mushrooms, paprika, salt and pepper. Cook mixture 2 minutes.

FROSTED MACADAMIA NUT SOUFFLE

1 quart macadamia nut ice cream
1 ounce dark rum
4 tablespoons whipped cream
4 teaspoons shaved macadamia nuts

1. Line edges of 4 soufflé cups with ¼" waxed paper borders.
2. Mix ice cream with rum in a chilled bowl. Fill soufflé cups with the mixture to ¼" above paper borders.
3. Freeze until solid. Before serving, remove paper borders. Garnish with whipped cream and macadamia nuts.

MATTEO'S

Dinner for Six

Minestrone alla Milanese

Matteo's Special Salad

Veal Saltimbocca Florentine

Cannoli

Espresso and Sambuca Romano

Wine:
C. K. Mondavi Zinfandel

Wanda Fusco, Owner

MATTEO'S

Matteo's is a gourmet's delight and a gourmand's heaven. If, on occasion, you would like to dine with celebrities such as Senator Robert Dole, Joe DiMaggio, Clint Eastwood, Mike Conners, Gerald Ford and a score of other regulars, this is the place to make your reservation.

Owner Wanda (Mrs. Nick) Fusco, a University of California at Los Angeles graduate, has an enviable background. She comes from a family of restaurateurs with establishments in Beverly Hills and Newport Beach, California. Mrs. Fusco is also an experienced publicist, having worked in a public relations capacity for Capitol Records.

About nine years ago Wanda learned of a prospective restaurant site in Honolulu. She investigated it thoroughly and, finding it to be a superior property, leased it. Mrs. Fusco named the establishment Matteo's and, thanks to her restaurant experience and public relations know-how, the new Matteo's became an Island favorite almost before you could say "fettuccine."

Wanda continues to maintain a test kitchen at home and has there developed some of Matteo's popular dishes, including the famous Chicken Wanda. Such diligent searching for innovative dishes is as laudable as it is rare.

While the capable young Micronesian chef, Theodore Decherong, uses his talents in Matteo's kitchen, Wanda's affable and indispensable husband, Nick, oversees the entire operation. Nick Fusco is the official tester and taster. He also sees to it that all stations are running smoothly.

364 Seaside Avenue
Honolulu

MINESTRONE ALLA MILANESE

½ cup olive oil
4 carrots, coarsely diced
1 stalk celery, diced
1 onion, diced
1½ quarts chicken stock
Salt to taste
½ teaspoon Accent
4 zucchini, diced
1 small head cabbage, coarsely chopped
1 cup ditalini pasta

1. Heat olive oil in a soup pot over medium heat. Add carrots, celery and onion. Sauté until onion is transparent.
2. Stir in chicken stock, preferably with a long-handled wooden spoon. Add salt and Accent. Slowly bring to a boil.
3. When a rolling boil is reached, turn off heat. Add zucchini, cabbage and ditalini.
4. Cover pot and let sit for 15 minutes.

The zucchini and cabbage will cook to perfection in the hot broth but will retain their texture.

MATTEO'S SPECIAL SALAD

2 heads iceberg lettuce
1 head romaine
½ pound salami
2 cups canned garbanzo beans
½ pound mozzarella cheese, grated
Salad Dressing

1. Wash lettuce and shake off as much water as possible without bruising it.
2. Break lettuce into a salad bowl roomy enough to toss the salad.
3. Dice salami and drain garbanzos. Add both to lettuce in bowl and mix thoroughly.
4. Sprinkle cheese over top. Add dressing to taste and gently toss all together.

Salad Dressing

1 cup olive oil
½ cup red wine vinegar
1 teaspoon Accent
1 teaspoon minced garlic
½ teaspoon oregano
Ground black pepper and salt to taste

Put all ingredients in mixing bowl and whip briskly with wire whisk.

VEAL SALTIMBOCCA FLORENTINE

2 bunches fresh spinach
3 pounds boneless veal steak
½ cup salad oil
½ cup all-purpose flour
1 quart brown sauce (see index)
6 thin slices prosciutto ham
6 thin slices mozzarella cheese
1 cup grated Parmesan cheese

1. Wash spinach thoroughly under cold running water. Remove tough stems and place in a pan with 3 to 4 tablespoons water. Boil 1½ to 2 minutes while turning and stirring with a fork.
2. Drain and chop. Approximately 2 cups should result.
3. Place veal between sheets of waxed paper and pound to pancake thickness with a tenderizing mallet. Cut into 6 portions.
4. Heat oil in a skillet over medium-high burner. Dust veal lightly with flour and place in hot oil for 10 seconds on each side. Remove with slotted spatula and allow to cool.
5. Cover the bottom of a large flat oven-proof pan with 2 cups brown sauce and distribute spinach over this. Place veal slices over spinach and cover with remaining sauce.
6. Place a slice of ham over each piece of veal and cover with a slice of mozzarella cheese.
7. Preheat broiler.
8. Sprinkle Parmesan over entire dish. Bring veal/sauce mixture to boil over medium-low heat, then melt Parmesan under broiler.

CANNOLI

1 cup all-purpose flour, plus enough extra to flour
   board
¾ cup granulated sugar
½ teaspoon ground cinnamon
1 egg yolk
¾ cup Marsala wine
Cannoli Filling

1. Put flour, sugar, cinnamon, egg yolk and wine into a mixer bowl and beat until well blended—about 1½ minutes.
2. Flour a breadboard or spread waxed paper over working area and flour it. Roll out dough as thin as possible, turning board and sprinkling dough with a little flour as you go.
3. Cut into approximately 3" squares.
4. Heat oil very hot in a french fryer or deep skillet.
5. Roll each dough square diagonally into a tube shape, using the handle of a wooden spoon or any other small round object as a mold. Press the overlap to seal.
6. Deep-fry 30 seconds and drain on paper towels.
7. Place **Cannoli Filling** in a pastry bag and fill shells.

Cannoli Filling

1 cup Ricotta cheese
¾ cup candied fruit mix
½ teaspoon vanilla extract
½ cup powdered sugar

Place all ingredients in mixer bowl and mix at medium speed.

SAMBUCA ROMANA LIQUORE CLASSICO

Sambuca Romana
18 to 24 roasted coffee beans of your choice

1. Fill 6 pony glasses with Sambuca Romana.
2. Float 3 or 4 whole coffee beans in each glass.
3. Flame 10 seconds to warm. Stir to blend coffee bean
   flavor with liqueur.

Sip slowly and allow the essence to cleanse the palate and remove any lingering food tastes. The coffee beans may be eaten or discarded.

MAUNA KEA
BEACH HOTEL

Dinner for Six

Turtle Soup Lady Curzon

Filet of Dover Sole Joinville

Medallions of Lamb Mascotte

Broiled Tomatoes

Artichoke Bottoms with Béarnaise

Château Potatoes

Butter Lettuce with Brie Cheese, Lemon Oil Dressing

Pear Suchard

Wines:

With Hors d'Oeuvres and Soup—Auxey-Duresses,
Ropiteau Frères, 1978
With Sole—Chablis Grand Cru, Les Clos, 1977
With Medallions of Lamb—Château Pichon-Longueville
Pauillac, 1969
With Dessert—Champagne, Perrier-Jouët, 1977

Kim Dietrich, Chef Executif
John Thomas, Maître d'Hôtel
Rosie Tayan and Douglas Caldwell, Wine Stewards

When the Mauna Kea Beach Hotel opened sixteen years ago, fanfare was royal and criticism tended towards the panegyric. The location on the big island of Hawaii is idyllic, the 310 rooms and suites are luxuriant, and golf, tennis, hiking, hunting and swimming are there to be enjoyed or disdained as fancy dictates. The staff-to-guest ratio of better than two-to-one ensures that the most spoiled of visitors will find himself pleasantly indulged in the midst of this veritable paradise.

Considering the quality of the accommodations, it should be no surprise that equal attention was lavished on the hotel's restaurants. What may be surprising, however, is that the dining rooms of the Mauna Kea have not merely exceeded the original high expectations, but are continually gathering new honors to an all-conquering reputation.

Executive Chef Kim Dietrich is currently secretary of the National Resort Food Executive Committee and a member of the American Culinary Federation, the American Academy of Chefs and the Confrérie de la Chaine des Rôtisseurs. After an apprenticeship in Germany and further experience in Switzerland, he emigrated to the United States. He has been with the Mauna Kea since 1971 and has brought the *Travel/Holiday* Award to the Pavilion Dining Room for the last five years.

Recently Chef Dietrich and his staff hosted a meal for the Hawaii chapter of the prestigious Chaine des Rôtisseurs, served when that brotherhood was gathered for a meeting at the Mauna Kea. The menu was quite favorably received, and Chef Dietrich has been kind enough to share those recipes in the following pages.

Mauna Kea Beach Hotel
Kamuela, Hawaii

HORS D'OEUVRES PLATE

1 (6-ounce) lobster tail
Mayonnaise
6 canned white asparagus spears
6 (½-ounce) slices Westphalian ham
3 canned or fresh raw quail eggs
6 (½-ounce) slices smoked salmon
6 thin slices **Roulade de Foie Gras
   in Port Wine Aspic** (see next page)
Parsley sprigs
Cherry tomatoes

1. Poach the lobster tail in its shell in salted water or court bouillon for
   15 minutes. Remove from heat and allow to cool in the poaching
   liquid. Push meat from shell intact and slice in 6 pieces. Arrange on
   one end of an attractive platter and garnish with mayonnaise. Reserve
   shell for **Sauce Joinville.**
2. Roll asparagus spears in ham slices. Place on platter.
3. Hard-boil quail eggs in water 10 minutes. Cool, shell and cut in half.
   Roll salmon slices and arrange on platter, garnishing each with half a
   quail egg.
4. Arrange slices of roulade in aspic on the platter.
5. Garnish platter with parsley sprigs and cherry tomatoes. Refrigerate
   until ready to serve.

Roulade de Foie Gras in Port Wine Aspic

1 pound knuckle veal
4 tablespoons butter
1½ pounds beef bones
1½ pounds veal bones
1 carrot, trimmed and sliced
1 onion, peeled and sliced
1 leek, trimmed and sliced
1 gallon water
¼ pound bacon rind
3 calf's feet
3 egg whites, beaten well
½ pound ground beef
1 bay leaf
2 cloves
2 tablespoons chopped parsley
Salt and pepper to taste
¾ cup port wine
6 ounces pâté de foie gras

1. Tie knuckle veal with string. Melt butter in a large pan and lightly brown knuckle veal and beef and veal bones. Transfer to a large stock pot and reserve pan.
2. Add carrot, onion and leek to meat in stock pot. Add water and bring to a boil.
3. Deglaze the first browning pan with water and add to stock pot. Skim off surface scum.
4. Tie bacon rind with string and add to pot, along with calf's feet. Simmer gently 5 to 6 hours. Strain.
5. Cool stock and remove hardened fat.
6. Mix egg whites and ground beef together. Stir into cooled stock. Tie bay leaf, cloves and parsley in a 4" square of cheesecloth and add to stock. Bring back to boil, stirring constantly. Simmer ½ hour.
7. Strain through muslin. Add port and season to taste with salt and pepper.
8. Pour a layer of aspic into a 10" pie pan. Chill to set.
9. Cut pâté into 6 slices and place evenly over chilled aspic. Pour another layer of aspic over and chill again to set.
10. Use a round or scalloped cookie cutter to cut out servings around pâté slices.

Aspic may be made in a pinch using canned consommé and gelatin, or even a packaged aspic powder. The wine may be added just before setting.

Any leftover aspic should be chilled, not frozen; it keeps well.

TURTLE SOUP LADY CURZON

½ cup whipping cream
1 teaspoon curry powder
2 teaspoons chopped mango chutney
2 (18-ounce) cans clear turtle soup

1. Whip cream until stiff.
2. Pre-heat broiler.
3. Add curry powder and chutney to cream. Blend thoroughly.
4. Heat soup and pour into serving bowls.
5. Put 1 heaping tablespoon whipped cream mixture on top of each bowl and glaze under hot broiler. Serve immediately.

In glazing the whipped cream topping, the broiler rack should be placed at its highest point so that the cream almost touches the flame. The glazing takes only a few seconds so it will necessitate your full attention.

FILET OF DOVER SOLE JOINVILLE

2 (16 to 20-ounce) Dover sole
1/8 pound shrimp
1/8 pound mushrooms
1 shallot, minced
1 clove garlic, minced
4 tablespoons butter
1 cup Chablis
Sauce Joinville
Fleurons

1. Skin and bone fish and cut into 8 filets. Reserve bones for stock.
2. Flatten 6 filets slightly with the side of a heavy knife or cleaver.
3. Mince remaining 2 filets with shrimp and mushrooms.
4. Sauté minced shallot and garlic in 1 tablespoon butter and add to shrimp mixture. Spread this mixture on the 6 filets and roll them up.
5. Melt 2 tablespoons butter in a sauté pan and add filets. Pour in Chablis, cover and cook 10 minutes over medium-low heat on stove, or in a 350° oven.
6. Remove fish carefully and keep warm. Reserve liquid for use in **Sauce Joinville.**
7. When sauce is finished, pour over filets. Garnish with **Fleurons.**

Sauce Joinville

Lobster shell and body (from Hors
    d'Oeuvres Plate)
1 tablespoon chopped carrot
1 tablespoon chopped celery
1 tablespoon chopped onion
1 tablespoon butter
Fish Stock
Salt and white pepper to taste
1 tablespoon brandy
1 cup heavy cream

1. Chop the lobster shell and body. Brown with chopped carrot, celery, onion and butter in a 350° oven.
2. Remove from oven and blend in flour.

3. Add *Fish Stock* and liquid from sauté pan. Season with salt and white pepper and add brandy. Simmer until well blended, then strain.
4. Add cream and reduce over low heat to a medium-thick consistency.
5. Adjust seasoning as necessary.

Fish Stock

¼ cup finely chopped onion
Sprig of parsley
Sprig of thyme
Bones and trimmings from sole
¼ teaspoon lemon juice
¼ teaspoon salt
2 cups water
½ cup dry white wine

1. Put onion, parsley and thyme in a pan and cover with fish bones and trimmings.
2. Add lemon juice, salt, water and wine.
3. Bring to a boil, skim and simmer gently 30 minutes.
4. Strain through muslin or a fine sieve.

An excellent brand of fish base is put out by Minor and may be substituted to save time.

Fleurons

3 cups sifted flour
1½ teaspoons salt
1 pound softened butter
1 cup water

1. Preheat oven to 400°.
2. Sift together the flour and salt. Make a well in the center and add the butter and water. Combine thoroughly.
3. Roll out dough and fold 2 sides in to meet at the center.
4. Fold in half top-to-bottom, making 4 layers.
5. Roll out again and repeat process 3 more times.
6. After fourth folding, roll out dough to about ⅛" thickness. Cut in half-moon shapes with a cookie cutter.
7. Bake 15 minutes in preheated oven.

We suggest serving a sorbet or spoom [see index] between the Filet of Dover Sole Joinville and the Medallions of Lamb Mascotte. This cleanses and refreshes the palate. In olden days a sweet liqueur was served to the same purpose, but sorbet is lighter, cooler, and refreshes better.

MEDALLIONS OF LAMB MASCOTTE

2 (30-ounce) racks of lamb
12 slices bacon
Jus

1. Bone lamb racks and set aside bones, to be used in preparing **Jus**.
2. Cut lamb into 12 (2½ to 3-ounce) portions. Shape and pat into round medallions.
3. Wrap a bacon slice around each medallion and secure with a toothpick.
4. Sauté to preferred doneness. Serve 2 per person with **Jus** on the side.

Jus

Bones from lamb racks
½ cup chopped celery
½ cup chopped onion
½ cup chopped carrot
½ cup white wine
1 cube beef bouillon
1 cup water

1. Brown the bones in a medium oven.
2. Dissolve the bouillon in the water. Add, along with chopped vegetables and wine, to browned bones. Simmer over low heat.
3. Deglaze pan used to sauté lamb medallions and add drippings to bones.
4. Reduce to about ½ cup liquid. Strain.

BROILED TOMATOES

6 firm ripe tomatoes
4 tablespoons butter, melted

1. Scald tomatoes in boiling water 1 minute.
2. Plunge into cold water to loosen skins. Remove skins.
3. Brush with melted butter.
4. Broil 5 to 6 minutes. Serve immediately.

ARTICHOKE BOTTOMS WITH BEARNAISE

2 tablespoons chopped tarragon
2 tablespoons chopped chervil
¼ cup tarragon vinegar
¼ cup white wine
1 tablespoon chopped shallot
⅛ teaspoon thyme
¼ bay leaf
½ teaspoon salt, or to taste
2 egg yolks
¼ pound sweet butter
Pinch of cayenne (optional)
6 artichoke bottoms, canned or
    freshly cooked

1. Put 1 tablespoon each of tarragon and chervil in a saucepan. Add vinegar and wine and see that the herbs are well-moistened. Add the shallots, thyme and bay leaf and place over medium-low heat.
2. Add salt; reduce liquid by two-thirds. Remove from heat and allow to cool.
3. Whisk 1 tablespoon water into the egg yolks and add to herb mixture. Place over very low heat and begin to beat strenuously with a wire whisk.
4. As the yolks begin to thicken, dribble the butter in slowly, while continuing to whisk, to incorporate.
5. Add cayenne and test for seasoning, adjusting if necessary.
6. Strain. Stir in remaining tarragon and chervil. Keep warm in a double boiler until ready to use.
7. To serve, spoon béarnaise onto artichoke bottoms.

CHATEAU POTATOES

3 large baking potatoes
2½ tablespoons butter
Salt to taste
½ cup chopped parsley

1. Using a melon baller, scoop out the potatoes to the size of large olives.
2. Parboil 7 to 8 minutes. Drain.
3. Heat the butter in a sauté pan and sauté potatoes, shaking pan occasionally, until tender and nicely browned.
4. Season with salt and garnish with chopped parsley.

BUTTER LETTUCE WITH BRIE CHEESE, LEMON OIL DRESSING

2 heads butter lettuce
6 ounces French Brie cheese
Lemon Oil Dressing
Watercress for garnish

1. Core lettuce heads and cut each into 3 wedges. Cut Brie into 6 slices.
2. Place lettuce wedges and cheese on individual salad plates. Spoon dressing over lettuce and garnish with watercress.

Lemon Oil Dressing

¼ cup freshly-squeezed lemon juice.
¾ cup salad oil
Salt and pepper to taste

Put the lemon juice in a bowl and add the oil slowly, beating constantly with a wire whisk until well blended. Add salt and pepper to taste.

PEAR SUCHARD

6 fresh pears
3 cups water
1½ cups sugar
4 ounces Grand Marnier
2 cups crushed coconut macaroons
12 ounces semi-sweet chocolate

1. Peel the pears but leave some skin around stems.
2. Make a simple syrup by combining the sugar and water and boiling over low heat until the syrup forms thin threads when dropped onto waxed paper.
3. Stir in 2 ounces Grand Marnier. Add pears and poach 1½ minutes. Leave in syrup but remove from heat. Marinate overnight.
4. Remove pears from syrup. Remove cores from the bottom, making sure to leave stem intact.
5. Mix crushed macaroons with remaining Grand Marnier. Fill pears with mixture.
6. Melt chocolate in a double boiler. Spoon over pears, coating each thoroughly but leaving the stems clear.
7. Chill to harden coating.

Dinner for Six

Oysters Casino

Boston Clam Chowder

Baked Stuffed Shrimp

Broccoli and Cherry Tomatoes Romano

Strawberry Crêpes

Wine:
Muscadet

Edward C. Greene, Proprietor
Jay J. Geffert, Head Chef

Located in Merchant Square amidst a blend of well-preserved vintage buildings that stand as an example of early Honolulu architecture, the Merchant Square Oyster Bar sits at the foot of Nuuanu Avenue. Adjacent to the lively pace of the Honolulu business district, the Oyster Bar bustles with activity during lunch as diners discuss business, celebrate special occasions, gather with friends, or make new acquaintances in the congenial style of a San Francisco seafood restaurant.

Intimate booths surrounded with live Boston ferns offer just the right amount of privacy, while blue-checkered tables offer space for large parties in a room separated by antique etched-glass doors. The most thrilling room of all, however, is the delightful garden courtyard set beneath a banyan tree, ringed with ferns and encircled by a colorful blue scalloped awning.

The restaurant serves a wide variety of seafood from the freshest of oysters, Dungeness crab flown in from San Francisco and fresh steamed clams from the Pacific Northwest, to scallops, shrimp and always-fresh local or mainland fish prepared a number of different ways. In addition, the menu selections are complemented by an excellent wine list offering choices from European and California vineyards.

Chef Jay Geffert has made the Oyster Bar in Merchant Square an oasis for seafood lovers and one of the most popular downtown luncheon spas. Geffert studied at the Culinary Institute of America in New York and worked in many East Coast restaurants as well as running his own catering business. He has created an exquisite menu at the Oyster Bar, including Seafood Canneloni and Oyster Sauté.

923 Nuuanu Avenue
Honolulu

OYSTERS CASINO

24 fresh bluepoint oysters
1 tablespoon finely chopped bell pepper
1 tablespoon finely chopped onion
½ teaspoon finely chopped parsley
¼ teaspoon garlic powder
½ pound butter, softened
Juice of ½ lemon
8 strips bacon, cut into thirds
Lemon wedges
Fresh parsley sprigs

1. Open oysters and separate meat from shells, placing meat on larger shell halves.
2. Sprinkle some rock salt on a large oven-proof serving platter and set oysters on top. Preheat broiler.
3. Combine bell pepper, onion, parsley and garlic powder with softened butter until smooth and creamy.
4. Top each oyster with ½ teaspoon herb butter and 2 drops lemon juice. Place one piece of bacon to completely cover each oyster and its herb butter.
5. Broil 4 to 5 minutes, or until bacon is bubbling and crisp. Garnish with lemon wedges and parsley.

The rock salt serves as a base to hold the oysters in place on the platter as well as retaining heat while serving.

BOSTON CLAM CHOWDER

2 strips bacon
1 medium-sized onion, diced
2 stalks celery, diced
2 tablespoons finely chopped parsley
½ pound frozen chopped clams
1 (8-ounce) can clam juice
2 medium-sized potatoes, diced ½"
½ teaspoon white pepper
1 quart milk
1 pint heavy cream
1 ounce dry sherry
1 tablespoon cornstarch

1. Fry bacon until crisp in a heavy-bottomed saucepan. Remove bacon and retain fat.
2. Lightly sauté onion, celery and parsley in bacon fat.
3. Add clams, clam juice, potatoes and white pepper. Simmer 15 to 20 minutes or until potatoes are tender.
4. Add milk and cream and bring to a boil.
5. In a separate cup, combine sherry and cornstarch. Slowly stir mixture into chowder to thicken. As it starts to boil, remove from heat.
6. Ladle into soup bowls. Crumble bacon over and serve immediately.

BAKED STUFFED SHRIMP

1 stalk celery, diced
½ onion, diced
1 tablespoon finely chopped parsley
6 tablespoons butter, melted
½ pound king crab meat, chopped
½ teaspoon salt
½ teaspoon pepper
4 slices sourdough bread, toasted and cut
    into small pieces
¼ pound WisPride Cheddar cheese
18 large shrimp
Hollandaise Sauce (see next page)
Parsley flakes

1. Preheat oven to 450°.
2. Sauté celery, onion and parsley in 2 tablespoons butter until soft.
3. Remove from heat and add crab, salt, pepper and bread. Mix
    thoroughly, adding cheese gradually.
4. Butterfly shrimp: With a sharp knife, cut down the back and just
    through the meat to the bottom shell. Remove the meat from shell
    but don't separate from the tail.
5. Stuff shrimp with crab mixture, about 3 tablespoons per shrimp. Use
    your hands to press firmly together and mold stuffed shrimp so
    they're plump and round.
6. Brush with remaining melted butter and bake in preheated oven for
    8 to 10 minutes.
7. Top with **Hollandaise Sauce** and parsley flakes.

*Garnish may also be simply a sprinkling of paprika, instead of
Hollandaise and parsley.*

*Stuffing can be made ahead and refrigerated until needed; or shrimp
can be stuffed ahead and refrigerated until ready to bake.*

MERCHANT SQUARE OYSTER BAR

Hollandaise Sauce

3 egg yolks
Juice of 1 lemon
Dash of cayenne pepper
½ pound butter, clarified
2 teaspoons warm water

Place egg yolks, lemon juice and pepper in a blender. Blend at high speed, slowly adding butter and water until rich and creamy.

For best results, prepare just before serving. The sauce separates if refrigerated or reheated.

BROCCOLI AND CHERRY TOMATOES ROMANO

1 pound broccoli
12 cherry tomatoes, halved
6 tablespoons butter, melted
Salt and pepper to taste
¼ cup freshly grated Romano cheese

1. Steam broccoli until tender.
2. Arrange on a serving platter with cherry tomatoes. Lace with melted butter and sprinkle with salt and pepper.
3. Top with Romano cheese. Keep warm until served.

It is best to cook broccoli just before serving so as to retain its bright green color.

STRAWBERRY CREPES

1 egg
1 cup milk
¼ teaspoon salt
½ teaspoon finely grated lemon peel
¼ cup flour
Strawberry Filling
Cheese Topping
Nutmeg

1. Beat egg. Stir in milk, salt and lemon peel. Sift in flour while beating vigorously until lumps have dissolved. Chill at least 2 hours.
2. Heat an oiled skillet. Ladle a small amount of batter into skillet; rotate pan to spread a thin film of batter over bottom. Cook both sides over medium-high heat. Repeat until batter is gone.
3. Place a portion of **Strawberry Filling** on each crêpe and roll. Place crêpes seam downward on individual dessert plates. Crown with **Cheese Topping**. Garnish with a dash of nutmeg.

Strawberry Filling

½ pound fresh strawberries
3 tablespoons Grand Marnier liqueur
2 tablespoons sugar

Clean and slice strawberries. Place in a bowl and pour liqueur over, then sprinkle with sugar.

Cheese Topping

6 ounces cream cheese
3 ounces sour cream
¼ teaspoon vanilla extract
¼ cup sugar
1 egg

Mix ingredients at high speed until thick and creamy or until all lumps have disappeared.

Michel's

Dinner for Four

Opakapaka Poche au Champagne Veronique

Spinach Salad
with
Michel's Special Dressing

Roast Loin of Veal

Braised Leeks

Carrots in Cointreau-Butter Sauce

Soufflé Glacé Grand Marnier

Wines:
With Fish and Salad—Mâcon Blanc
With Veal—Puligny-Montrachet
With Soufflé—Château d'Yquem, Sauternes

Gordon William Hopkins, Chef
Robert Clark, Maître d'
Karl Gonda and Alfred Wan, Wine Stewards

When Michel's opened May 5, 1961 at the Colony Surf Hotel, with Michel Martin at the helm, it was an immediate success. Monsieur Michel has gone on to other ventures but the restaurant that bears his name continues to garner dining's most coveted awards under the guidance of Master Chef Gordon William Hopkins.

Oahu-born Hopkins' dining background includes training periods with an enviable array of fine restaurants: Ernie's in San Francisco, Scandia in Beverly Hills, Cincinnati's La Maisonette, Chicago's Whitehall Club —and on to Michel's in 1975. This twenty-seven-year-old chef has worked with thirteen master chefs! His own credo: "Sauces must be light and act as a complement, not a cover-up; easy on the seasonings—let foods retain their natural flavors; keep vegetables slightly undercooked; and combine traditional wisdom with knowledge of new techniques."

Along with its award-winning cuisine, Michel's setting is lovely. Nestled on the beach at the foot of Diamond Head, the view is spectacular: to witness the sunset from this site is an experience that's rarely forgotten.

2895 Kalakama Avenue
Honolulu

OPAKAPAKA POCHE AU CHAMPAGNE VERONIQUE

4 to 5 pounds fresh opakapaka, scaled and
  cleaned
2 tablespoons butter or margarine
2 tablespoons chopped shallots or green onions
½ cup finely chopped fresh mushrooms
½ cup champagne
½ cup dry white wine
½ cup **Fish Stock** (see next page)
¼ cup whipping cream
½ cup **Velouté de Poisson** (see next page)
¼ cup **Hollandaise Sauce** (see second page following)
½ cup seedless green grapes

1. Preheat oven to 350°.
2. Cut opakapaka into 15 to 20 boneless filets, each weighing about 3
   ounces. Reserve head and carcass to make **Fish Stock.**
3. Melt butter with shallots or green onions and mushrooms over low
   heat for about 1 minute in a large oven-proof skillet.
4. Add champagne, white wine, **Fish Stock** and fish filets. Cover and
   bake in preheated oven for 10 minutes.
5. Remove skillet from oven, carefully remove fish filets from skillet
   and place filets on serving tray. Set aside.
6. Add whipping cream and **Velouté de Poisson** to skillet containing
   liquid in which fish was poached. Simmer 10 minutes or until sauce
   has reached desired thickness.
7. Remove from heat and stir in **Hollandaise Sauce.**
8. Add grapes and mix well. Pour sauce over fish filets and serve.

Note: Most restaurants have a pot filled with fish stock and pre-made
sauces, ready for use. At home, you'll have to start from scratch by
making the **Fish Stock,** the **Velouté de Poisson** (fish sauce) and the
Hollandaise Sauce before even beginning the main recipe for the poached
fish. To make things easier, make the **Fish Stock** and the **Velouté** the
day before you expect to serve the dish.

Fish Stock

Makes ½ gallon.

1 to 2 pounds fish bones and trimmings
 (use reserved opakapaka trimmings, or
 other fish may be substituted)
1 gallon water
1 stalk celery, chopped
1 onion, chopped
1 bay leaf,
1 teaspoon white pepper
Pinch of rosemary
Pinch of thyme

1. Place fish bones and trimmings in water and bring to a boil.
2. Add remaining ingredients. Allow to simmer 4 to 5 hours, until broth is reduced by half. Strain.

Velouté de Poisson

4 tablespoons butter or margarine
2 teaspoons chopped shallots or green onions
2 tablespoons flour
¼ cup sliced mushrooms
½ cup dry white wine, plus more as needed
1½ quarts **Fish Stock**, plus more as needed
1½ cups whipping cream
Salt and pepper to taste

1. Melt 2 tablespoons butter in a small saucepan.
2. Add 1 teaspoon shallots or green onions and cook for about 30 seconds.
3. Add flour and cook for 2 minutes, stirring constantly. Do not allow the flour to brown. Set aside.
4. Melt remaining 2 tablespoons butter in a large pot.
5. Add remaining shallots or green onions and mushrooms and cook for 30 seconds. Do not allow to brown.

6. Add wine and fish stock. Simmer for approximately 25 minutes or until mixture is reduced by half.
7. Add flour/butter mixture.
8. Add whipping cream and beat constantly until sauce thickens. If sauce is too thick dilute with a little more white wine.
9. Simmer 20 minutes more, beating constantly. If sauce becomes too thick, dilute with a little more **Fish Stock.**
10. Taste for seasoning, adding salt and pepper as desired.
11. Strain sauce through a sieve, discarding mushrooms and shallots.

Hollandaise Sauce

2 tablespoons dry white wine
5 shallots, chopped
Dash of lemon juice
2 dashes Tabasco sauce
2 dashes Worcestershire sauce
6 tablespoons warm clarified butter
2 egg yolks
Salt and white pepper to taste

1. Mix white wine, shallots, lemon juice, Tabasco and Worcestershire sauce in a small saucepan. Simmer over low heat for 1 to 2 minutes.
2. Place saucepan over a pot half filled with water, or over bottom half of a double boiler, at simmer.
3. Add egg yolks and beat constantly for 3 to 4 minutes or until sauce thickens. Be careful: if the mixture gets too hot, the egg yolks will curdle.
4. Remove saucepan from heat. Add clarified butter in a slow, steady stream, beating constantly, until sauce is of desired thickness. Taste for seasoning.

Note: To clarify butter, place in a small saucepan over low heat. Allow butter to melt and skim off solids from surface. Use only the clear liquid.

SPINACH SALAD

3 slices bacon
2 bunches young, tender Horenso (mainland)
   spinach
Spinach Dressing
Salt and black pepper
2 hard-cooked egg whites, very finely chopped

1. Cook bacon. Drain fat, reserving 3 tablespoons for **Spinach Dressing,** and chop bacon.
2. Wash spinach thoroughly and remove tough stems. Shake dry and place in a large wooden bowl.
3. Heat **Spinach Dressing** to boiling. Pour over spinach and toss lightly until leaves are slightly wilted.
4. Salt and pepper to taste. Garnish with chopped egg whites and bacon. Serve immediately.

Spinach Dressing

1 cup *Michel's Dressing*
3 tablespoons bacon fat
2 teaspoons chopped chives
2 tablespoons red wine vinegar
1½ tablespoons brown sugar

Combine ingredients in a blender.

Michel's Dressing

¼ teaspoon Dijon mustard
¼ teaspoon salt
½ teaspoon white pepper
Scant ¼ teaspoon parsley juice
Scant ¼ teaspoon Aromat seasoning
½ teaspoon garlic powder
¼ teaspoon Maggi sauce
1 teaspoon Worcestershire sauce
3 tablespoons red wine vinegar
3 tablespoons olive oil
6½ tablespoons cottonseed oil

1. Combine first 9 ingredients in a blender.
2. Add oils and mix well.

ROAST LOIN OF VEAL

4 tablespoons butter
½ cup flour
2 pounds strip loin of veal, well trimmed
Salt and pepper to taste
3 sprigs fresh thyme
Cognac Crème Sauce (see next page)

1. Preheat oven to 350°.
2. Melt butter in an oven-proof pan over medium-high heat.
3. Lightly flour veal and sauté on both sides until it begins to brown. Season with salt, pepper and thyme.
4. Bake 10 minutes in preheated oven.
5. Remove veal from pan and keep warm. Reserve pan for **Cognac Crème Sauce.**
6. To serve, place veal on a serving platter. Slice on the bias, very thinly. Ladle **Cognac Crème Sauce** onto each dinner plate, placing veal slices on top.

Cognac Crème Sauce

½ cup veal stock or beef consommé
¼ cup Courvoisier
¾ cup demi-glace (veal or beef stock reduced
    by ½)
¼ cup heavy cream
Salt and pepper to taste
Few grains cayenne papper
¼ teaspoon chopped fresh parsley

1. Pour off fat from veal pan. Heat pan so it is very hot, without
   burning the drippings. Add veal stock, Courvoisier and demi-glace.
2. Reduce liquid at low temperature until slightly thickened.
3. Add cream, salt, pepper, cayenne and parsley.
4. Bring to slow boil. Reduce heat and simmer to a rich creamy
   consistency.
5. Place in a gravy boat or sauce bowl and serve at table.

BRAISED LEEKS

8 leeks
6 tablespoons butter
1 cup chicken broth
¼ cup finely chopped parsley
½ green pepper, finely chopped
¼ teaspoon nutmeg
¼ teaspoon thyme
Salt and white pepper to taste

1. Preheat oven to 350°.
2. Trim green tops and root ends off leaks. Remove outer layer and wash
   each leek separately and thoroughly under running water. (They are
   inclined to retain dirt between layers so get as much water as possible
   between these layers.)
3. Shake out the water and wipe dry on paper towels.
4. Melt butter in a shallow baking dish and arrange leeks side by side in
   the pan.
5. Add chicken broth, chopped parsley, green pepper, nutmeg, thyme,
   salt and white pepper.
6. Cover dish and bake in preheated oven for 30 minutes, or until leeks
   are tender.

CARROTS IN COINTREAU-BUTTER SAUCE

2 bunches young carrots
2 tablespoons butter
Salt and white pepper to taste
5 tablespoons honey
2 tablespoons Cointreau

1. Preheat oven to 350°.
2. Wash and peel carrots. Cut into diagonal slices.
3. Steam slices until tender—about 12 minutes.
4. Place slices in a heated bowl and add butter, salt, pepper and honey.
   Stir so that each slice has a butter shine.
5. Spoon Cointreau over.

Note: If the carrots are small enough, do not peel them and slice only once.

SOUFFLE GLACE GRAND MARNIER

5 eggs
½ cup granulated sugar
3 ounces Grand Marnier
¾ cup whipping cream
Fresh raspberries or strawberries for garnish
2 fresh mint leaves
Powdered chocolate

1. Fill the lower part of double boiler two-thirds full of water and bring
   almost to boil. Keep on a heat that will maintain that temperature.
2. Place a large stainless steel mixing bowl over the bottom pan. Add
   eggs, sugar and Grand Marnier. Whip with a wire whisk until it has
   the consistency of Hollandaise sauce. (This will take some time—5 to
   15 minutes, depending upon the weather.)
3. Remove the bowl from heat and set into a bowl of crushed ice.
   Continue whipping until the mixture cools.
4. Whip cream in separate bowl until very thick.
5. Slowly fold whipped cream into egg mixture with a rubber spatula.
6. Cut a 6" wide strip of butcher paper or waxed paper to fit around
   the top of a 1-quart soufflé dish. Secure it with a rubber band, making
   a 4½" collar above the dish. Pour mixture into dish.
7. Freeze overnight.
8. Before serving, remove paper collar and garnish with raspberries or
   strawberries, mint leaves and a sprinkling of powdered chocolate.

Nick's Fishmarket
Hawaii · Beverly Hills · Chicago

Dinner for Six

King Crab Meat and Shrimp Scampi Combination

Greek Salad

Roast Chicken Oregano, Greek Style

Zucchini Amandine

Chocolate Crème de Menthe Cake

Wine:
With Chicken—Puligny-Montrachet, Le Cailleret, 1977

Jeff Harmon and Nick Nicholas, Owners
Eddie Fernandez, Head Chef
Hans Van Rennes, Maître d'

It is quite true that great food is the main enticement in building a restaurant's clientele, but to soar to the heights of Nick's Fishmarket and to keep those customers coming back demands a great deal more.

Although the recent acquisition of Nick's by local restaurateur Rex Chandler (former owner of Rex's Restaurante) was intentionally underplayed, it came with the assurance that no sweeping changes would be made. Rex did not acquire Nick's Fishmarket with the idea of upgrading it (that would be like trying to improve on the Mona Lisa) but will, with certainty, see that all the award-winning qualities are maintained.

To quote Rex, "I believe in the principle of fine dining in an atmosphere of comfort and privacy, and will continue to feature a complete menu of over fifty fresh seafood entrées, supplemented by the finest in beef, veal and chicken dishes."

There is booth seating with individual customer-controlled rheostat lights and a telephone jack in each booth so one doesn't have to go stumbling about to find a way to check with the baby sitter. There are tuxedoed waiters, a six-year-veteran maître d' (whose previous training included hotel management in Europe), a jazz group in the lounge, original oils by Hawaii's noted abstract artist, John Young, valet parking and an extensive wine list with more than a hundred selections.

And then there is the chef. For eleven years, youthful and energetic Eddie Fernandez has spurred his staff into the daily accomplishment of meeting gastronomic demands of one hundred seventy diners per sitting, straight through the busy dinner hours until one-thirty in the morning. Having worked up from broiler cook to head chef, Fernandez is quite adept at directing such a demanding operation—and it shows. Awards include *Institutions* magazine's 1980 Emmy award for one of four top restaurants in the United States.

Waikiki Gateway Hotel
2070 Kalakaua Avenue
Honolulu

KING CRAB MEAT AND SHRIMP SCAMPI COMBINATION

12 large shrimp, peeled and deveined
6 Alaskan king crab legs
Garlic Butter

1. Butterfly the shrimp and lay them flat in an oven-proof pan or skillet. Broil for about 1 minute.
2. Brush crab legs with **Garlic Butter** and add to pan. Cook for 2 minutes over a medium-low burner.
3. Arrange on a platter, alternating 2 shrimp to each crab leg.

Garlic Butter

¼ pound butter
5 to 6 cloves garlic, minced
½ teaspoon salt
½ tablespoon chopped parsley
2 to 3 drops Tabasco sauce
⅛ teaspoon Lea & Perrins
    Worcestershire sauce
⅛ cup brandy
⅛ cup sauterne

Place all ingredients in a blender and mix well.

GREEK SALAD

1 medium head romaine lettuce
1 medium head iceberg lettuce
1 small head chicory
1 cup olive oil
½ cup red wine vinegar
1 tablespoon oregano
½ teaspoon sugar
1 small onion, julienned
12 Greek olives
10 ounces feta cheese
12 anchovy filets
1 large tomato, cut into 6 wedges
6 radishes
6 small sprigs watercress
1 lemon, cut into 6 wedges

1. Cut romaine, iceberg and chicory into bite-size pieces. Rinse
   thoroughly and spin in a wire salad basket or pat dry on paper towels.
2. Mix oil, vinegar, oregano and sugar in a large bowl. Whisk well.
3. Add lettuce, onion and feta cheese. Toss gently but thoroughly.
4. Serve on individual plates and garnish with anchovies, tomato,
   radishes, watercress and lemon wedges.

ROAST CHICKEN OREGANO (Greek Style)

3 fryers, halved (and boned, if desired)
½ cup olive oil
6 tablespoons lemon juice
1½ tablespoons salt
1 tablespoon MSG
1 tablespoon pepper
¾ cup oregano
2 tablespoons paprika
¾ pound butter

1. Preheat oven to 400°.
2. Arrange half-chickens skin side up in an oven-proof baking dish.
3. Sprinkle or brush on oil and lemon juice.
4. Shake on—in order—salt, MSG, pepper, oregano and paprika.
5. Place small pats of butter evenly over chickens. Bake uncovered in preheated oven 15 to 20 minutes, basting at least every 5 minutes.

ZUCCHINI AMANDINE

2 medium zucchini
3 eggs
1 cup flour
1 cup olive oil
¾ cup butter
2 tablespoons blanched almonds

1. Wash and trim zucchini. Slice about ¼" thick.
2. Beat eggs lightly in a bowl.
3. Spread zucchini slices out on a piece of waxed paper and dust both sides with flour.
4. Heat olive oil in a skillet until very hot. Dip floured zucchini slices in egg and drop in the hot oil. Sauté until brown on both sides.
5. Drain oil and add butter and almonds. Cook only until butter is browned.
6. Drain and serve immediately.

CHOCOLATE CREME DE MENTHE CAKE

1 (8" or 9") White Cake
1 pint whipping cream
2 ounces crème de menthe
1 cup grated sweet Baker's chocolate
1 cup chocolate chips

1. Cut cake into 3 layers using a very thin, sharp knife.
2. Whip cream until stiff, adding crème de menthe a little at a time.
3. Blend in grated chocolate.
4. Assemble cake, icing well between layers with the whipped cream. Coat outside evenly with remaining icing and decorate with chocolate chips.

White Cake

3 cups all-purpose flour
¼ teaspoon salt
½ teaspoon baking soda
½ teaspoon baking powder
4 eggs
½ pound butter
2 cups sugar
1 teaspoon vanilla extract
1 teaspoon lemon extract

1. Preheat oven to 325°.
2. Sift together flour, salt, baking soda and baking powder.
3. Beat eggs, butter, sugar, vanilla and lemon extract with a whisk or an electric beater at high speed until batter is fluffy.
4. Turn the beater to medium speed (or continue with wire whisk) and mix in flour until batter is smooth.
5. Grease an 8" or 9" round spring-form cake pan with Crisco and lightly sprinkle with flour. Pour in batter and bake in preheated oven 1 hour.
6. Allow cake to cool before cutting and decorating.

The Peacock RESTAURANT

Dinner for Four

Poisson Cru

Turtle Soup Anglaise

Hearts of Palm Chablisienne

Lapin Chasseur

Young Spring Carrot

Baked Papaya Gauguin

Wine:
With Lapin—Mirassou Zinfandel

Green Meadows, Inc., Owners
Kevin Knox, Manager
Charles F. Lee, Chef
Craig Parker, Maître d'

The Peacock restaurant is situated atop a grassy rise above the Kaanapali Beach Hotel, just off Maui's main highway. From almost any point in the dining room, on the spectacular lanai or even from the luxuriant bar, one looks out over an impeccably-maintained golf course to an endless expanse of blue-green ocean.

Of course, the sheer natural beauty of Maui, impressive as it is, could not of itself make a superior restaurant. Great care was taken to achieve a harmonious design for the Peacock. Terry Jones-Haber was engaged to decorate; he gathered silks and brass from Thailand, hand-painted china from Hong Kong and exquisite rattan furniture from the Philippines.

Still, a restaurant's enduring fame rests on more than ambience. The ideal of fine dining has always meant superb food in complementary surroundings, and in the end it is the kitchen arts that establish a reputation. And, in a bare two years, the efforts of Chef Charles F. Lee and Food and Beverage Controller Kevin Knox have earned the Peacock a remarkably well-founded reputation. One reason for this is the care and skill of the kitchen staff; another is the quality of the ingredients used. For example, for their Lapin Chasseur (rabbit cooked in white wine with mushrooms and herbs), a herd of rabbits are specially kept on a farm in Haiku (Maui). They are dressed for the Peacock while still quite young, averaging two to two-and-a-half pounds, and thus are very tender and succulent.

The Peacock's parent company, Green Meadows, Inc., also owns and operates the Quail Lodge in Carmel, California—a Mobil Five-Star hotel —and the Carmel Valley Golf and Country Club. The Peacock's amiable Chef Lee was formerly at the Quail and, prior to that, at the Fishhouse on the Park, also in Carmel.

2560 Kekaa Drive
Kaanapali Beach, Lahaina, Maui

POISSON CRU

½ pound fresh ahi (bluefin tuna)
1 tablespoon salt
1 cup fresh lime juice
1 large ripe tomato, finely diced
1 small Maui onion, finely diced
¼ cup celery, finely diced
½ cucumber, finely diced
2 scallions, finely diced
1 clove garlic, finely diced
⅛ teaspoon white pepper, or to taste
1 (12-ounce) can coconut milk

1. Cut fish into ½" cubes.
2. Mix salt and lime juice, add fish, stir and marinate in refrigerator 2 hours.
3. Combine tomato, onion, celery, cucumber, scallions and garlic.
4. Remove fish from lime juice and drain well.
5. Combine fish with vegetables and add white pepper to taste.
6. Blend in coconut milk and mix thoroughly.
7. Serve well chilled.

If Maui onions are not available use sweet, yellow Texas onions. Select one that is more flat than round—it will be sweeter.

TURTLE SOUP ANGLAISE

1 pound turtle meat
1 bay leaf
¼ teaspoon thyme
¼ teaspoon rosemary
½ pound butter
2 stalks celery, diced
2 medium onions, diced
4 small carrots, diced
1 cup sherry
1 quart beef stock or prepared beef broth
⅔ cup flour
½ pint half-and-half
¼ teaspoon white pepper, or to taste

1. In a large soup kettle, combine turtle meat with 2 quarts water.
2. Put bay leaf, thyme and rosemary in a piece of cheesecloth and tie it with a piece of strong thread, making a bouquet garni. Add this to soup kettle.
3. Cook 1 hour over medium heat. Remove meat, chop finely and set aside.
4. Strain stock through cheesecloth or a fine sieve.
5. In a 4-quart dutch oven, bring ¼ pound butter to sizzle over medium heat and sauté celery, onion and carrots.
6. Add sherry and bring to a boil.
7. Add turtle stock, beef stock and turtle meat. Return to a slow boil.
8. Make a roux by melting remaining butter and mixing in flour. Whip into hot broth to thicken; simmer ½ hour.
9. Stir in half-and-half, add white pepper to taste and serve.

HEARTS OF PALM

1 (12-ounce) can hearts of palm
1 head romaine lettuce
2 tomatoes, sliced
Dressing
1 tablespoon chopped parsley

1. Slice hearts of palm lengthwise into quarters.
2. Arrange a bed of romaine on a serving plate or bowl. Spread tomato slices on top.
3. Crisscross with strips of palm.
4. Dress salad and garnish with chopped parsley.

Dressing

1 tablespoon Dijon mustard
½ tablespoon sugar
2 tablespoons wine vinegar
1 cup salad oil
⅛ teaspoon thyme
⅛ teaspoon marjoram
1 bay leaf
White pepper to taste

1. Combine mustard, sugar and vinegar.
2. Slowly dribble in salad oil while beating vigorously.
3. Add spices.

LAPIN CHASSEUR

2 large carrots, peeled and quartered
    lengthwise
1 stalk celery, sliced diagonally in 5 or 6
    pieces
1 large onion, peeled and quartered
½ cup peanut oil
Flour
1½ cups white wine
2 tablespoons tomato paste
1 quart chicken stock or canned chicken
    broth
½ teaspoon thyme
1 bay leaf
½ teaspoon ground rosemary
3 tablespoons salt
Seasoned salt to taste
Pepper to taste
½ pound mushrooms, quartered
2 small rabbits, sectioned into 12 pieces
1½ tablespoons oyster sauce

1. Using a large, flameproof casserole, sauté carrots, celery and onion in
   2 tablespoons oil until tender.
2. Stir in 3 tablespoons flour until smooth and add wine.
3. Blend in tomato paste and chicken stock.
4. Add spices and mushrooms. Bring to a slow boil and simmer ½ hour,
   stirring occasionally.
5. Preheat oven to 350°.
6. While stock is simmering, flour the rabbit pieces and sauté in 6
   tablespoons peanut oil until lightly browned. Place in the simmering
   casserole.
7. Add oyster sauce, cover and bake 40 to 45 minutes in preheated oven.

Oyster sauce may be found in the Asian foods sections of most markets.

YOUNG SPRING CARROTS

12 small young carrots
Salt
White pepper
2 tablespoons sweet butter
2 tablespoons finely chopped parsley

1. Wash carrots and trim off tops. (True baby carrots should not be peeled.)
2. Place whole in a saucepan holding enough salted water to generously cover the bottom of the pan. Boil over medium heat just until tender— about 15 minutes. Test with a fork and keep watching that the water does not evaporate completely. Add more water if necessary.
3. When done, remove from the pan with a slotted spoon. Add pepper to taste and coat with butter. Garnish with chopped parsley.

BAKED PAPAYA GAUGUIN

2 ripe papayas, halved and seeded
2 tablespoons brown sugar
1 tablespoon white rum
2 tablespoons coconut syrup
½ cup shredded coconut
2 cups whipped cream

1. Preheat oven to 350°.
2. Place halved papayas on baking sheet.
3. Combine sugar, rum and coconut syrup. Spoon mixture over papayas.
4. Sprinkle with shredded coconut.
5. Bake 15 minutes in preheated oven.
6. Allow papayas to cool a bit, then top with freshly whipped cream and serve.

Pearl City Tavern
HAWAII

Dinner for Six

Shrimp Bisque

Greek Salad

Stuffed Maine Lobster

Sabayon

Wine:

Crustace Alsace

Tomio Maeda, Owner
Ken Mihara, General Manager and Director
Richard Nieto, Chef

Pearl City Tavern, 15 miles west of Honolulu, has been in operation for twenty years. It is one of the "must see" places on the island, especially if one is doing the full circle. It is not only an oasis for the motoring tourist but is a favorite meeting place for the locals as well.

Only the mischievous antics of the enchanting squirrel monkeys in the bar could momentarily hold one back from plunging directly into the culinary triumphs of Chef Richard Nieto. The diminutive monkeys are the first thing one sees upon entering. A former Pearl City Tavern owner brought a few over from South America several years ago and built a large glassed-in area for them behind the bar. Animal lovers will be glad to know the monkeys are obviously happy; they breed well and live to a ripe old age. There are now twelve of the active little fellows and over the years they have become so popular that any time Pearl City Tavern is mentioned, someone invariably says, "Sure, that's the place with the monkey bar!"

Pearl City Tavern's cheery, almost festive air draws a constant flow of customers. Fortunately its two large dining rooms have a combined seating capacity of 270, so there is usually no waiting for a table. Chef Nieto, a youthful and dedicated cook, is certainly equal to the challenge of the popular dinner house. Nieto was lured to the Tavern in 1978. Prior to that he gained valuable experience at the Kahala Hilton Hotel —a most prestigious training ground.

Chef Nieto, along with general manager and director Harry Umemoto, must be doing something right: year after year more tourists keep pouring into the Pearl City Tavern, while the local clientele remains constant. Surely they're not all coming back just to see the monkeys!

905 Kamehameha Highway
Pearl City, Oahu

SHRIMP BISQUE

¼ pound butter
½ cup finely diced celery
½ cup finely diced onion
1 cup sliced fresh mushrooms
1 cup diced shrimp
1 pint fish stock
Scant ½ cup flour
1 pint whole milk, warm
½ cup tomato purée
Salt and pepper to taste
2 to 3 tablespoons sherry, or to taste

1. Heat half the butter in a non-stick skillet until it bubbles.
2. Add celery, onion, mushrooms and shrimp. Sauté only until the onions are clear and the celery a little pliable.
3. Add fish stock.
4. Melt the other half of the butter in a 2-quart saucepan and stir in the flour to make a roux.
5. Add the warm milk, stirring constantly until the mixture thickens and is thoroughly blended.
6. Combine with the fish stock mixture, tomato purée, salt and pepper. If too thick, correct with a bit more milk.
7. Splash in the sherry and serve hot.

GREEK SALAD

1 medium head iceberg lettuce
1 small head Manoa or butter lettuce
1 large cucumber
½ cup sliced black olives
Salt and pepper to taste
Italian dressing
2 tablespoons grated Parmesan cheese
1 hard-cooked egg, chopped

1. Thoroughly wash the lettuce and shake out excess water or drain on paper towels. Cut into thin strips.
2. Peel the cucumber. Quarter it lengthwise, then cut into lengths of about 1¼".
3. Put the lettuce and cucumber in a roomy wooden salad bowl. Toss in the olives, salt, pepper and dressing.
4. Garnish with Parmesan cheese and the chopped egg.

This is one salad for which the lettuce should be cut, not torn. If you use a knife with a stainless steel blade, the lettuce won't discolor.

STUFFED MAINE LOBSTER

6 (1¼-pound) Maine lobsters
1 cup diced celery
1 cup diced onion
1 cup cubed scallops
1 cup diced Bay shrimp
½ cup crab meat
4 tablespoons butter
Salt and ground black pepper
¼ teaspoon MSG
¼ cup sherry
1¼ cups mayonnaise
6 teaspoons cracker meal

1. Preheat oven to 350°.
2. Immerse lobsters in boiling salted water for 5 to 7 minutes and let cool in the same water.

3. While they're cooling, sauté celery, onion, scallops, shrimp and crab meat in butter. Season to taste with salt and pepper.
4. Add MSG and sherry. Strain mixture to release excess liquid.
5. While this mixture is draining, if lobsters have cooled sufficiently, place them belly side up on a cutting board. Cut them down the middle with a sharp knife and open them flat, leaving the meat intact.
6. Remove the stuffing mixture from the strainer to a bowl. Add the mayonnaise and stir gently until well mixed.
7. Mound filling on each lobster shell. Sprinkle cracker meal over the tops. Bake 5 to 7 minutes in preheated oven until golden brown.

Note: If Bay shrimp are unavailable, another kind will do.

In Hawaii, rice is our staple and is a perfect complement to fish in any form. Because of the richness of this lobster dish, we suggest plain boiled (or steamed) long-grain rice, served in separate bowls.

SABAYON

2 oranges
2 lemons
6 egg yolks
1½ cups granulated sugar
½ cup red wine
½ cup white wine
¼ cup sherry
1 quart French vanilla ice cream
24 ripe strawberries

1. Extract juice from the oranges and lemons.
2. Grate the rinds on a piece of waxed paper or in a small bowl.
3. In the top of a double boiler over water just under boiling, beat egg yolks for 1 minute.
4. Add grated orange and lemon rinds and all other ingredients except ice cream and strawberries.
5. Keep beating until mixture attains the consistency of Hollandaise sauce and foams up a bit. Remove from heat.
6. Make individual strawberry sundaes and liberally top with the sauce.

LA PEROUSE

Dinner for Four

Tahitian Poisson Cru

Palace Court Salad

Papaya Seed Dressing

Steak La Perouse

Parisienne Potatoes

La Perouse Stir-Fry Vegetables

Raspberry Flambé

Wines:
With Poisson Cru and Salad—Robert Mondavi Fumé
Blanc, 1972
With Steak—Robert Mondavi Cabernet Sauvignon,
1973

Werner Boettner, Executive Chef
Josef Augustin, Restaurant Manager

The Compte de la Perouse was a derring-do French explorer and seafarer who left his name and deeds indelibly stamped on the memory of the southwest coast of Maui. He was neither a pirate nor a do-gooder, but an artful trader who, in 1786, plied his trade (and trades) with such distinction it was decreed the beautiful bay wherein he anchored should bear his name.

In 1976, the oceanfront Hotel Intercontinental opened its doors—and simultaneously it opened those of the truly lovely and sophisticated La Perouse restaurant. The decor is wonderfully exotic in its lavish display of oriental silk tapestries, porcelain vases and urns, cooling stone pools and African artifacts. The food, like the atmosphere in which it is served, is stunning.

An incredible integration of flavors results when Executive Chef Werner Boettner and Restaurant Manager Joseph Augustin skillfully blend the exotic with the simple, the Continental with the local, the other-worldly with the earthy. For example, one might begin with an appetizer of Italian Prosciutto with Kiwi Fruit—that sweet gooseberry-like delight from New Zealand. For a satisfying soup course one should try Boula Boula, a creamy turtle-and-split-pea combination. Then on to a favorite Hawaiian entrée, Baked Pulehu Fish, seasoned with rock salt and coconut oil, wrapped with seaweed and baked in a ti leaf.

Chef Boettner, a native of Germany, was graduated from the Wiesbaden Hotel Institute and received his training at two of Europe's finest hotel restaurants, the Nassauer Hof in Wiesbaden and the Breidenbacher in Dusseldorf. Some of the most highly regarded kitchens in London, Toronto and Vancouver, B.C. have since experienced his artistry. In 1976 Chef Boettner received the highest accreditation conferred by the elite American Culinary Federation.

Even though 139 persons may dine simultaneously at La Perouse, the room will never feel that full. With its intimately arranged tables and booths, rich koa wood paneling, plush suede upholstery and subdued lighting by candle lamps, La Perouse has a quiet elegance that is a perfect atmosphere for distinguished dining. *United Mainliner* certainly agrees, having given the establishment its Excellence in Dining award for 1980.

Hotel Intercontinental
Wailea, Maui

TAHITIAN POISSON CRU

1 pound fresh white fish filet
1 bell pepper, cut in thin strips
½ onion, chopped
Juice of 1 lemon
Juice of 4 limes
1 cup ketchup
1 cup diced pimientos
Tabasco sauce to taste
Salt and freshly ground black pepper
    to taste

1. Cut fish in pencil-thin strips.
2. Place fish, bell peppers and onions in a dish or bowl. Pour lemon and lime juices over, seeing that all pieces are saturated.
3. Marinate 2 hours in refrigerator.
4. Remove from refrigerator and combine with remaining ingredients.

This must be kept very cold and is especially good if served in crystal bowls that fit over crushed ice.

PALACE COURT SALAD

2 heads Manoa lettuce
1 rounded cup Bay shrimp
Salt and pepper
Juice of ½ lemon
1 tablespoon olive oil
1 tablespoon red wine vinegar
3 tablespoons **Papaya Seed Dressing**
¼ cup chopped hard-cooked egg yolk
¼ cup chopped parsley
1 tomato, cut into 4 wedges
4 snow crab legs, cooked (usually available
   cooked in fish markets)

1. Wash lettuce and remove excess moisture. Break by hand.
2. Sprinkle Bay shrimp with salt, pepper and lemon juice. Toss in a
   bowl with olive oil and vinegar.
3. Add **Papaya Seed Dressing**. Gently fold in lettuce. Sprinkle with egg
   yolk and parsley.
4. Garnish with tomato wedges and crab legs.

Note: Because of its fragile nature, Manoa lettuce is not transportable.
So, on the Mainland, use any lettuce to your taste.

Papaya Seed Dressing

1 rounded tablespoon finely chopped onion
½ teaspoon freshly squeezed ginger juice
1 clove garlic, finely chopped
½ teaspoon dry mustard
1 tablespoon lemon juice
¼ teaspoon ground black pepper
½ teaspoon salt
1 teaspoon tarragon
2 tablespoons chopped fresh papaya seeds
2 cups oil

Put all ingredients in bowl and beat well with wire whisk.

*Pour any leftover dressing into a glass jar and store in refrigerator for
future use. It probably won't be there very long, but it does keep well.*

STEAK LA PEROUSE

4 (10-ounce) New York steaks
Salt to taste
4 tablespoons unsalted butter
¼ cup finely chopped shallots
2 tablespoons green Madagascar peppercorns
¼ teaspoon ground marjoram
¼ teaspoon ground thyme
¼ teaspoon ground rosemary
1 ounce Courvoisier
1 ounce dry red wine
¼ cup brown sauce (see index)
¼ cup unsweetened whipped cream.

1. Lightly salt steaks.
2. Bring butter to high heat in a heavy skillet, but be careful not to burn. Sauté steaks until half done.
3. Add shallots, peppercorns and spices and flame with Courvoisier.
4. Remove steaks from pan and keep warm.
5. Add wine to pan. Reduce liquid by half. Add brown sauce and remove pan from heat.
6. Fold in whipped cream.
7. Pour sauce over steaks and serve.

PARISIENNE POTATOES

2 large baking potatoes
¼ cup clarified butter
Salt
Parsley sprigs

1. Peel and rinse potatoes. Scoop out rounds with a melon baller.
2. Rinse potato balls, place in a pan of lightly salted water and bring to a boil.
3. Reduce heat and simmer 1 minute.
4. Drain, wash in cold water and dry on paper towels.
5. Sauté in clarified butter over low heat until golden brown. Sprinkle with salt to taste.
6. Garnish with parsley sprigs and serve on a heated dish.

Note: An average baking potato will yield 15 to 20 balls, so figure 7 to 10 per person.

LA PEROUSE STIR-FRY VEGETABLES

2 stalks celery
2 stalks broccoli, stems only
1 carrot
1 small horseradish (2" to 3")
1 small yellow onion, coarsely chopped
¼ small cauliflower, broken into florets
1 tablespoon peanut oil
1 teaspoon dill weed
Salt and pepper to taste

1. Wash all vegetables thoroughly in cold water.
2. Slice celery, broccoli stems, carrot and horseradish diagonally into thin strips.
3. Using a wok or large sturdy skillet, heat peanut oil over medium-high heat.
4. When oil is hot, add vegetables and stir so all are exposed evenly to heat and oil.
5. Immediately add dill weed and salt and pepper.
6. Continue to stir vegetables. Cook no more than 3 minutes.

RASPBERRY FLAMBE

4 teaspoons granulated sugar
4 teaspoons unsalted butter
1½ cups fresh raspberries
1 ounce Pernod
Juice of 2 medium oranges, strained
Juice of 1 medium lemon, strained
1 tablespoon dry red wine
1 tablespoon Cointreau
4 scoops vanilla ice cream

1. Heat a skillet over high heat and caramelize sugar, stirring constantly.
2. Add butter, making sure not to burn it.
3. Quickly add raspberries and flame with Pernod.
4. When burnt off, add juices, wine and Cointreau.
5. Serve over vanilla ice cream.

This recipe works equally well with blackberries and boysenberries.

Dinner for Four

Lobster-Crab Cocktail

Maui Onion Soup

Spinach Salad with Pernod

Tenderloins of Beef Rudyard Kipling

Sabayon de Amaretto

Wines:

With Lobster and Salad—a Chablis Premier Cru, 1976
With Tenderloins—La Tache, 1974
With Sabayon—Château d'Yquem, Sauternes, 1970

Neil Sint Nicolaas, Executive Chef
Johnathan Robinette, Chef de Cuisine
Paul Sanford, Maître d'
Tony Eichers, Assistant Maître d'

The very mention of Raffles' conjures up visions of Singapore slings, hot curry dishes and international spies jockeying for position at the bar. The ambience here evokes intrigues and adventure and one expects to find Peter Lorre in a corner booth and Humphrey Bogart muttering "Play it again, Sam" to the pianist.

Raffles' is named as a salute to the original in "Casablanca," but the charm and ambience of the Maui version make it truly unique. It is frequented by a lively, suntanned gathering of honeymoon couples, executives on vacation, businesspeople from neighboring islands and locals who have come to know and appreciate the satisfaction of a superlative dinner. International, yes, but it's the Hawaiian flavor that makes it irresistible.

Hawaiian Colonial and Far Eastern in decor, Raffles' is set on two levels, allowing every diner a sweeping view of its flower gardens with the Pacific Ocean immediately beyond. There is charming, unobtrusive piano —skillfully played by Hawaii's own Martin Denny—confined mainly to the lounge area. On evenings when the trade winds are most balmy the sliding glass doors are opened wide to admit their caress.

Executive Chef Neil Sint Nicolaas served his apprenticeship in Holland, then continued on to London, Scotland and the United States mainland. Nicolaas has skillfully served Western International Hotels in various parts of the world for the past thirteen years. For Raffles' grand opening in 1978, Chef Nicolaas was called in to design and execute a menu sufficiently varied and imaginative to gratify gourmet and neophyte alike.

Wailea Beach Hotel
Wailea, Maui

LOBSTER-CRAB COCKTAIL

1 large lemon
1 tablespoon salt
2 (6-ounce) lobster tails
16 snow crab legs
¼ head lettuce, shredded
Parsley sprigs
Caviar and Brandy Sauce

1. Halve the lemon. Slice one half into 5 wedges. Squeeze juice of 1 wedge into a pan of water and add 1 tablespoon salt. Bring to a rapid boil over high heat.
2. Add lobster and crab and boil 15 minutes. Remove, allow to cool and extract meat from shells.
3. Place the lettuce in a bowl and squeeze the half lemon over. Toss lightly and arrange as beds in champagne glasses.
4. Slice lobster tails into 8 pieces each. Arrange 4 pieces lobster and 4 crab legs over each bed of lettuce. Make cuts in the remaining lemon wedges and place on rims of glasses.
5. Garnish with parsley sprigs. Serve accompanied by **Caviar and Brandy Sauce.**

Caviar and Brandy Sauce

2 cups mayonnaise
¼ cup drained horseradish
Juice of 1 lemon
½ cup brandy
½ cup ketchup or tomato sauce
1 ounce black caviar
Salt and pepper to taste

Mix all ingredients together in a bowl.

MAUI ONION SOUP

1 pound Maui or sweet Texas onions, sliced
2 tablespoons butter
1 quart beef stock or canned beef broth
¼ teaspoon thyme
¼ teaspoon marjoram
¼ teaspoon bay leaf
1½ tablespoons vinegar (omit if you do *not*
   use Maui onions)
½ cup white wine
Salt and pepper to taste

1. Peel and slice onions. Sauté in butter until lightly browned.
2. Add beef stock, spices, vinegar and wine.
3. Simmer gently 1 hour.
4. Adjust seasoning.

SPINACH SALAD WITH PERNOD

1½ pounds spinach
5 strips bacon
¼ pound mushrooms, sliced
1 ounce Pernod
1 cup Italian dressing
¼ cup Parmesan cheese·
Croutons

1. Snip leaves from spinach stems with thumbnail and wash under cold running water. Drain excess water on paper towels.
2. Sauté bacon until crisp; drain and crumble. Reserve fat.
3. Add mushrooms to bacon fat and sauté 2 to 3 minutes.
4. Flame with Pernod.
5. Stir in Italian dressing.
6. Heat to a boil and pour over spinach.
7. Add Parmesan cheese, bacon bits and croutons. Toss and serve immediately on hot plates.

TENDERLOINS OF BEEF RUDYARD KIPLING

8 (4-ounce) beef tenderloin steaks
8 strips bacon
¼ pound butter
½ pound mushrooms, quartered
1½ cups red wine
1½ cups **Brown Sauce**
¾ pound crab legs or crab meat, cooked
1½ cups **Béarnaise Sauce** (see second page following)

1. Wrap steaks with bacon strips and secure with toothpicks.
2. Heat butter in a heavy skillet over high flame and sauté steaks to individual liking. Remove from heat and keep warm.
3. Sauté mushrooms in the same pan. Add red wine and reduce heat.
4. Stir in **Brown Sauce**.
5. Briefly immerse crab meat in a small amount of boiling water to heat. Remove and drain.
6. Top 4 steaks with mushroom sauce and the other 4 with warm crab pieces and **Béarnaise Sauce**.

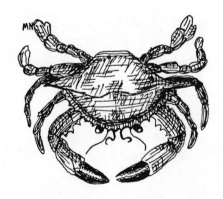

Brown Sauce

2 tablespoons butter
2 tablespoons flour
1 cup *Brown Meat Stock*
Salt and pepper to taste
A few drops Maggi sauce (optional)

1. In a small saucepan or skillet, melt butter over low flame. Add flour, stirring constantly, to make a smooth roux. Cook mixture until golden brown.
2. Gradually stir in meat stock, adding salt and pepper to taste.
3. If a darker color is desired, add a few drops of Maggi sauce.

Brown Meat Stock

If you buy bones, have your butcher crack them for you.

2 pounds beef bones with small amount of
   meat remaining on them
½ cup chopped onion
½ cup chopped celery
2 tablespoons chopped parsley
8 to 10 peppercorns
Salt to taste
1 quart water

1. Combine all ingredients in a soup kettle, cover with cold water and place over medium-low heat.
2. Slowly bring to a simmer. Adjust heat if it threatens to boil. Simmer all day, or at least 5 hours.
3. Remove bones and strain liquid.
4. Refrigerate overnight and remove fat.

Note: Add any leftover roast bones or steak bones or any bits and pieces of meat and/or vegetables to the stock pot for additional flavor.

If all is not used in a day or so, put the remainder in a glass jar and freeze.

Béarnaise Sauce

6 tablespoons tarragon vinegar
2 teaspoons finely chopped shallots or scallions
8 peppercorns, crushed
½ teaspoon chervil
2 teaspoons chopped parsley
¼ teaspoon mace
8 egg yolks
1 cup butter, softened
½ teaspoon tarragon
Salt to taste

1. Simmer vinegar, shallots or scallions, peppercorns, chervil, parsley and mace in a small saucepan over low heat. Reduce by half.
2. Strain through a fine sieve and add 2 tablespoons water.
3. Whip egg yolks in the top of a double boiler that has not yet been put over heat. (Have very hot but not boiling water ready in bottom of double boiler.)
4. Continue to whip egg yolks while slowly adding vinegar and herb mixture.
5. Stir in about one-fourth of the butter and place top of double boiler over bottom part. Heat it to just below boiling temperature.
6. Keep stirring and add remaining butter as mixture thickens to the consistency of heavy cream.
7. Remove top of double boiler from heat and stir in tarragon. Add salt to taste.

Note: Do not allow the top part of the double boiler to touch the hot water.

SABAYON DE AMARETTO

Break the eggs first and pick out a representative shell half for measuring the other ingredients. This will ensure the correct proportions.

6 egg yolks
1 egg shell of sugar
1 egg shell of white wine
1 egg shell of Amaretto liqueur
Fresh fruit in season

1. Whisk all ingredients together in a double boiler over hot but not boiling water. Continue whisking until mixture is thickened like custard.
2. Serve over fresh fruit in champagne glasses.

Take advantage of available fresh fruits such as bananas, strawberries, grapes, papayas, raspberries and the like.

THE SWAN COURT

Dinner for Six

Oysters Polynesia

Gazpacho

Nettings of the Hukilau

Macadamia Nut Cream Pie

Wines:

With Oysters and Gazpacho—Chappellet Chenin Blanc,
1977
With Nettings—Spring Mountain Chardonnay, 1978

Gordon Hentschel—General Manager
Heinrich Wiegmann—Executive Chef

The Swan Court Restaurant is aptly named. It boasts a large man-made lagoon adjacent to the ocean, inhabited by gliding swans, strutting penguins and colorful flamingos. During daylight hours it is a charming setting but after nightfall, with strategically placed lights playing over all, the scene is "storybook".

Millions of dollars have been invested in authentic pieces of statuary, many of which are quite massive. These are placed throughout the interior of the hotel as well as along paths and by-ways of the garden walks. Here, old world elegance and new world technology are contained with future world ease and pleasure. The Hyatt Regency is the new queen of Maui hotels, and her reign may be of some duration because it would take some two hundred million dollars to dethrone her.

It is not only one's eyes that are feasted here; Executive Chef Heinrick Wiegmann provides feasts for the palate as well. With more than twenty years experience in some of the finest hotels in Europe, the United States mainland and Hawaii, Chef Wiegmann's artistry is his ability to meld the best of traditional French, Polynesian and nouvelle cuisine— and thus please everyone.

Hyatt Regency Hotel
Lahaina, Maui

OYSTERS POLYNESIA

36 fresh bluepoint oysters, washed, shucked
  and on the half shell
1 medium onion
½ pound mushrooms
½ pound zucchini
¼ pound prosciutto ham
¼ medium pineapple
6 ounces **Curry Sauce** (see next page)
6 ounces Hollandaise sauce (see index)

1. Preheat oven to 350°.
2. Place oysters in half shells in a heat-resistant dish on a flat sheet pan.
3. Cut onion, mushrooms, zucchini and ham into fine julienne strips. Mix together and place a small amount of this mixture on top of each oyster.
4. Cut pineapple into fine juliennes and sprinkle over.
5. Spread 1 teaspoon curry sauce and 1 teaspoon Hollandaise on each oyster.
6. Place the sheet pan with oysters in preheated oven for approximately 8 minutes, or until top of sauce begins to brown.
7. If possible, place under broiler for the last minute to obtain a brown glaze on each oyster. Serve immediately.

Curry Sauce

¼ cup finely chopped onion
¼ cup finely chopped apple
¼ cup chopped or crushed pineapple
2 tablespoons finely chopped pear
2 tablespoons finely chopped banana
4 slices bacon, chopped
2 tablespoons butter
¼ cup flour
2 tablespoons curry powder
1 cup chicken stock
1 cup coconut milk
¼ cup mango chutney
Salt

1. Sauté onion, apple, pineapple, pear, banana and bacon in butter over medium heat until golden brown.
2. Blend in flour and curry powder. Cook 2 minutes.
3. Stir in stock, coconut milk and chutney. Reduce heat and simmer 1 hour.
4. Season to taste with salt.

This recipe makes approximately 2 cups. The unused portion can be frozen and used later with one cup of meat (chicken, shrimp, lamb or beef) for a main curry dish.

GAZPACHO

2 large tomatoes
1 large cucumber
1 medium onion
¼ avocado
½ medium green pepper
4½ cups tomato juice
⅓ cup olive oil
⅓ cup red vinegar
¼ teaspoon Tabasco sauce
2 teaspoons Worcestershire sauce
2 teaspoons fresh lemon juice
1½ teaspoons salt
⅛ teaspoon ground black pepper
6 celery stalks

1. Peel and dice tomatoes, cucumber, onion and avocado. Seed and dice green pepper. Refrigerate at least ½ hour.
2. Combine tomato juice, olive oil, vinegar, Tabasco sauce, Worcestershire sauce, lemon juice and seasonings. Mix well and chill.
3. Divide vegetables into each soup bowl or large bowl-style glass.
4. To serve, present a bowl to each guest and ladle the chilled tomato juice mixture into each until vegetables are three-quarters covered.
5. Garnish with celery stalks and serve.

THE NETTINGS OF THE HUKILAU

Red snapper, dolphin, grouper, swordfish or halibut filets work well.

Juice of 1 lemon
1 teaspoon Worcestershire sauce
6 fresh fish filets, approximately 6 ounces
    each
Salt and pepper to taste
½ cup all-purpose flour
½ pound unsalted butter
3 bunches fresh watercress, washed and
    trimmed
2 thumb-size portions fresh ginger root, peeled
    and finely chopped

1. Combine lemon juice and Worcestershire sauce. Thoroughly brush filets with mixture. Drain and save marinade.
2. Season fish to taste with salt and pepper. Flour well.
3. Using a pan large enough to hold all six filets, heat ¼ pound butter over medium heat.
4. Sauté filets until both sides are golden brown. Remove from heat.
5. Remove filets from pan and keep warm. Leave drippings in pan and add watercress. Stir until wilted, then remove and spread on heated platter to form bed for fish.
6. Arrange filets on watercress so they slightly overlap.
7. Add remainder of butter to the pan and place over medium heat until butter turns golden brown.
8. Add chopped ginger root and the marinade. Stir and distribute over filets. Serve immediately.

A lovely dish served alone—or accompanied by boiled new potatoes.

MACADAMIA NUT CREAM PIE

1 cup milk
3 tablespoons sugar
$1/8$ teaspoon salt
2 tablespoons butter
1 ounce unflavored gelatin
1 pint whipping cream, whipped
3 egg yolks, beaten
¼ cup macadamia nut liqueur or dark rum
1 (9") **Pie Crust**
6 to 8 chocolate-dipped macadamia nuts

1. Bring milk, sugar, salt, butter and gelatin to boil. Stir constantly to avoid burning the mixture. After reaching the boiling point, let mixture cool.
2. Reserve ¼ of the whipped cream; carefully fold egg yolks into the remainder.
3. Add liqueur and diced macadamia nuts while continuing to fold.
4. Thoroughly combine egg yolk-whipped cream mixture with cooked milk mixture and pour into **Pie Crust**. Let cool in refrigerator.
5. To serve, garnish each piece with remaining whipped cream and one chocolate-dipped macadamia nut.

Pie Crust

½ cup butter
½ cup margarine
2 cups flour
3 to 4 tablespoons ice water

1. Preheat oven to 350°.
2. Cut butter and margarine into flour with a knife or pastry blender until the texture resembles corn meal. Add ice water gradually, working in just enough to hold the dough together.
3. Roll out on a lightly floured board to 1" thickness.
4. Place in refrigerator for 20 minutes.
5. Roll out dough to fit $1/8$" thick in a 9" aluminum pie pan. Cut away excess dough and form a scalloped border.
6. Bake 15 minutes in preheated oven. Let shell cool before filling.

Dinner for Four

Asparagus Cream Soup

Seafood Potpourri

Filet Charlemagne

Braised Belgian Endive

Hot Raspberry Sauce with Vanilla Ice Cream

Wines:
With Seafood Potpourri—Piesporter Goldtröpfchen
Auslese
With Filet Charlemagne—Château Belgrave
Haut Médoc
With Dessert—Mumm's René Lalou

Siegfried Poesch, Manager
Klaus Saballus, Chef
Richard Dean, Sommelier
Donald L. Dickhens, General Manager

If the Taj Mahal had a dining room, one would expect it to look like the multi-award-winning Third Floor Restaurant, located in the Hawaiian Regent Hotel in Waikiki. Immediately upon entering, one feels one has left the world of mere mortals and entered a paradise flowing with exquisite trays of edible delicacies. The selection of pupus—Hawaiian for canapés or hors d'oeuvres—seems infinite; and if you have not lost control completely before the staggering dessert cart is brought to your table, do so then. Go on that diet tomorrow.

The Third Floor's Chef Klaus Saballus is a chef extraordinaire in many ways. He is German-born but following a thorough apprenticeship in Berlin, southern Germany and Switzerland, he began moving west. The Hotel Bonaventure in Montreal benefited from his talents before he continued on to San Francisco. Chef Saballus succumbed to the lure of Hawaii in 1973 and, after signing on with the Hawaiian Regent Hotel, has had no further inclination to roam. And why should he? The scores of delighted diners love him and the hotel gives him the freedom and encouragement to experiment with imaginative sauces, soups, entrées or whatever his agile mind dictates. Actually, Chef Saballus maintains a beautiful balance (particularly in the making of sauces) between his rich European heritage and nouvelle cuisine.

"Quality in cooking takes time and love. If you don't cook with love in your heart—if you don't truly enjoy it—even the finest recipe and the finest ingredients will fail to create great cuisine," says the wise Saballus. "This is not a restaurant to which you might go every night. It is a special place for special evenings.

"The menu which follows is not a menu you would cook every day. The ingredients are elegant, unusual and expensive. But, let me assure you, if you cook these dishes with love in your heart, you will experience pride and passion for the dish you have created. So cook with care, with creativity and with courage!"

Hawaiian Regent Hotel
2552 Kalakaua Avenue
Honolulu

ASPARAGUS CREAM SOUP

1 pound fresh asparagus
¼ cup butter
2 tablespoons flour
Juice of ½ lemon
Salt and pepper to taste
3 ounces Chablis
½ pint half-and-half, as needed

1. Peel and wash asparagus. Cook in boiling water for approximately 5 minutes, or until tender but still slightly crisp. Remove asparagus; strain off and reserve stock, adding enough water to make 4 cups.
2. Melt butter in a saucepan, add flour and stir in with a wire whisk.
3. Add asparagus stock and stir just until it starts to boil. Reduce heat and let simmer 15 to 20 minutes.
4. Add lemon juice, salt and pepper to taste. Stir in Chablis and continue to simmer another 10 minutes.
5. Thicken to taste with half-and-half.
6. Cut asparagus into 1" pieces and add to soup.
7. Taste for seasoning and texture, adjusting if necessary. Serve hot.

SEAFOOD POTPOURRI

¼ teaspoon salt
2 tablespoons lemon juice
8 large shrimp, peeled and deveined
4 crab claws, cooked
8 medium crab legs, cooked, shelled and
  cut in half
Cocktail Sauce
4 parsley sprigs
2 cherry tomatoes, halved
1 lemon, quartered

1. Bring 2 cups water to a rapid boil in a small saucepan. Add salt and lemon juice.
2. Boil shrimp 3 to 4 minutes, then remove with a slotted spoon and transfer to a bowl of ice water. This will keep them crisp.
3. Just before you are ready to serve, combine all seafoods attractively in individual glasses and cover with **Cocktail Sauce**.
4. Garnish each cocktail with a sprig of parsley, half a cherry tomato and a lemon wedge on the rim of glass.

Cocktail Sauce

4 egg yolks
1 teaspoon mustard—Grey Poupon is best
1 teaspoon white wine vinegar
1 teaspoon lemon juice
1 teaspoon salt
1 teaspoon white pepper
2 cups salad oil
2 teaspoons ketchup
1 teaspoon fresh shredded horseradish
Scant ⅛ teaspoon cayenne pepper
1 ounce brandy

1. Put egg yolks in a medium bowl and whisk for 1 minute.
2. Add mustard, vinegar, lemon juice, salt and pepper. Continue to whisk while dripping in oil drop by drop, as in making mayonnaise.
3. Add ketchup, horseradish, cayenne pepper and finally the brandy.
4. Whip to a good thick consistency.

FILET CHARLEMAGNE
ROASTED FILET OF TENDERLOIN

2 pounds beef tenderloin
Salt and pepper to taste
¼ to ½ teaspoon rosemary
¼ to ½ teaspoon thyme
2 tablespoons salad oil
Sauce Charlemagne

1. Preheat oven to 350°.
2. Season entire surface of tenderloin with a mixture of salt, pepper, rosemary and thyme.
3. Heat salad oil in a heavy oven-proof pan or skillet over medium-high heat. Brown meat on all sides.
4. Bake in preheated oven 25 to 30 minutes. Serve with **Sauce Charlemagne.**

Sauce Charlemagne

2 tablespoons fresh butter
½ cup Chablis
Juice of 1 lemon
1 pound fresh mushrooms, washed and quartered
2 tablespoons cornstarch
2 tablespoons water
½ pint half-and-half
Salt and pepper to taste

1. Place butter, Chablis and lemon juice in a small pan. Stir constantly while bringing to a boil.
2. Add mushrooms and turn heat down immediately. Cook 5 minutes over medium-low heat.
3. Remove mushrooms from broth and set aside.
4. Dissolve cornstarch in water and whisk into broth to thicken. Add mushrooms to the thickened sauce.
5. Blend in half-and-half until smooth.
6. Season with salt and pepper.

BRAISED BELGIAN ENDIVE

8 heads small Belgian endive
Butter
Salt and white pepper to taste

1. Preheat oven to 350°.
2. Wash endive and trim off ends.
3. Place in a buttered glass pie pan. Season with salt and white pepper to taste. Add 1 cup water and cover with foil.
4. Bake for 20 to 25 minutes in preheated oven.

HOT RASPBERRY SAUCE WITH VANILLA ICE CREAM

¼ cup granulated sugar
1 pint fresh raspberries
¼ cup red wine
1 teaspoon cornstarch
8 scoops vanilla ice cream

1. Place sugar, raspberries and 2 tablespoons wine in a small saucepan over medium heat. Stir until mixture starts to boil.
2. Mix remaining wine with cornstarch and add to raspberry paste. Let simmer 3 to 5 minutes.
3. Place ice cream in bowls. Cover with warm raspberry sauce. Serve immediately.

Dinner for Six

Creamed Avocado Soup Kamehameha

Willows Salad

Fresh Shrimp Curry

Sky-High Coconut Cream Pie

Wine:
Mâcon Lugny, Les Charmes

Bill Woo, General Manager

If you would like to host an authentic, traditional Hawaiian luau, it must be held at the Willows. Tree-lined, and in a garden setting of pure Hawaiiana, there is just no place on Oahu like it.

Prior to World War Two the property was known as Kapa'akea Springs, but when the McGuire-Hausten family purchased it thirty-six years ago, it was renamed the Willows and has been known by that ever since. The thatch-roofed restaurant rests serenely amid lush garden foliage with a waterfall, lagoon and fishpond stocked with rare multicolored carp. Strolling Hawaiian musicians serenade unobtrusively from six-thirty to nine-thirty every evening.

Recently, Randy M. Lee Jr., an entrepreneur many will remember as president/general manager of the beloved Halekalani Hotel, purchased the Willows. He promised all seventy-five employees and the public at large that all Willows traditions would remain intact—and so they have. One has a choice of eight seating areas: the King's Hale, Queen's Hale, Lagoon Hale, Palm Patio, Kukui Hale, Garden Court, Orchid Lounge or the Garden Pavilion, where a weekly Hawaiian poi luncheon is served each Thursday. In addition, breakfast and early morning meetings can be scheduled. Experience with the Willows management has proved that almost anything can be arranged. It is a "gracious symbol of old Hawaii."

901 Hausten Street
Honolulu

WILLOWS CREAMED AVOCADO SOUP KAMEHAMEHA

1 large ripe avocado
1 Maui or sweet Texas onion
1 quart half-and-half
2 tablespoons sherry
2 tablespoons Ajinamoto (optional)
Salt
Tabasco sauce to taste

1. Peel and slice avocado.
2. Peel onion and cut into blender. Purée with avocado until smooth.
3. While continuing to purée, add half-and-half slowly, followed by sherry, Ajinamoto (optional), salt and Tabasco sauce.
4. Strain and chill. Serve in very cold iced bowls.

WILLOWS SALAD

Fresh greens
Cucumber slices
Cherry tomatoes
Sliced mushrooms
Alfalfa sprouts
Bacon bits
Fresh chives
Willows House Dressing

1. Toss together all ingredients except bacon bits and chives.
2. Dress with **Willows House Dressing.**
3. Just before serving, garnish with bacon bits and chives.

Amount and combinations of above vegetables will depend upon seasonal availability and your own taste.

Willows House Dressing

2 teaspoons anchovy paste
½ tablespoon sugar
1 teaspoon tarragon vinegar
½ teaspoon red wine vinegar
½ teaspoon garlic purée
⅓ teaspoon finely chopped fresh parsley
¼ teaspoon finely chopped fresh green onion
½ cup milk
1⅓ cups mayonnaise

1. Mix all ingredients together except mayonnaise and milk, blending thoroughly.
2. Gradually add milk and then mayonnaise.
3. Chill and serve cold.

FRESH SHRIMP CURRY

36 to 48 medium-sized shrimp
1 tablespoon peanut oil
3 ounces white wine or dry vermouth
Salt and pepper to taste
3 level tablespoons curry powder
Willows Curry Sauce, heated

1. Wash, shell and devein shrimp. Using a good sharp knife, slice in half.
2. Marinate 15 to 20 minutes in oil, wine, salt and pepper.
3. Put curry powder in non-stick skillet over medium-low burner and let it come to low heat.
4. Remove shrimp from marinade with slotted spoon and put in skillet with dry curry powder.
5. Sauté about 5 minutes or until shrimp turns pink, turning 2 or 3 times.
6. Add to hot curry sauce and serve.

By first warming the dry curry powder, the subtleties of all the East Indian spices and herbs are accented and the flavors then permeate the shrimp as no other method of preparation could hope to do.

Willows Curry Sauce

6 tablespoons butter
3 cloves garlic, minced
3 slices fresh ginger root, finely chopped
3 small onions, finely chopped
1 tablespoon salt
1 tablespoon granulated sugar
3 tablespoons curry powder
8 to 10 tablespoons flour
2 quarts coconut milk

1. Melt butter in a large heavy saucepan over medium heat. Do not let it brown.
2. Stir in garlic, ginger and onion with a wooden spoon. Add salt, sugar, curry powder and flour. Mix thoroughly.
3. Dribble in coconut milk a little at a time, stirring to a smooth thickness. Simmer 20 minutes.
4. Allow to stand several hours. Strain before serving.

This curry sauce is also marvelous served with chicken.

WILLOWS RICE

1 cup long-grain rice
5 cups water
2 teaspoons salt

1. Run cold water over rice and rinse several times until milky white appearance begins to disappear. Drain.
2. Bring water and salt to a hard boil in a 2-quart saucepan. Gradually add rinsed and drained rice to pot, stirring constantly.
3. Cover. Reduce heat and simmer for 18 to 20 minutes or until rice is tender and all the water is absorbed.

APPLE-GLAZED CARROTS

2 cups sliced carrots
1½ tablespoons melted butter
3 tablespoons brown sugar
¼ cup applesauce

1. Blanch carrots lightly in boiling water. Drain well.
2. Preheat oven to 350°.
3. Combine butter, brown sugar and applesauce in a small saucepan. Cook over low heat, stirring, until brown sugar is melted.
4. Place carrots in a baking dish and pour applesauce mixture over.
5. Bake in preheated oven until heated through (10 to 15 minutes at most).

SKY-HIGH COCONUT CREAM PIE

3 cups scalded milk
1 tablespoon butter
½ cup granulated sugar
⅛ teaspoon salt
¼ cup grated fresh coconut
5 tablespoons cornstarch
4 egg yolks
¼ teaspoon vanilla
9" pie shell, cooled
Meringue
¼ cup fresh grated coconut

1. Preheat oven to 400°.
2. Combine milk, butter, sugar, salt and grated coconut in a 1-quart saucepan or double boiler. Let mixture come to near boil, stirring occasionally.
3. Mix cornstarch with enough water to make a medium paste. Add to hot milk and continue cooking until thickened, stirring continuously. When thickened, remove pan from heat.
4. Beat egg yolks until creamy. Slowly add a small amount of the hot mixture to eggs and blend fully.
5. Replace pan over low heat. Stir in egg mixture and vanilla and cook about 3 minutes more. Remove from heat and allow to cool.
6. Fill pie shell and top with **Meringue**. Sprinkle grated coconut over. Bake in preheated oven 10 minutes or until meringue is nicely browned. Let cool. Chill before serving.

Meringue

6 egg whites
½ teaspoon salt
¼ cup sugar
½ teaspoon vanilla

1. Beat egg whites and salt together until soft peaks form.
2. Gradually beat in sugar until meringue is smooth and stands firm.
3. Stir in vanilla.

A little stabilizer—such as ½ teaspoon cream of tartar or Xacto—may be added with the salt to help hold the meringue.

Entrees

DINING IN—THE GREAT CITIES

A Collection of Gourmet Recipes from the Finest Chefs in the Country

_____ Dining In—Baltimore   _____ Dining In—Pittsburgh

_____ Dining In—Boston   _____ Dining In—Portland

_____ Dining In—Chicago   _____ Dining In—St. Louis

_____ Dining In—Dallas   _____ Dining In—San Francisco

_____ Dining In—Hawaii   _____ Dining In—Seattle, Vol. II

_____ Dining In—Houston, Vol. I   _____ Dining In—Toronto

_____ Dining In—Houston, Vol. II

_____ Dining In—Kansas City

_____ Dining In—Los Angeles

_____ Dining In—Minneapolis/St. Paul   _____ Feasting In—Atlanta

_____ Dining In—Monterey Peninsula   _____ Feasting In—New Orleans

Forthcoming:

_____ Dining In—Denver   _____ Dining In—Sun Valley

_____ Dining In—Manhattan   _____ Dining In—Vancouver, B.C.

_____ Dining In—Philadelphia   _____ Dining In—Washington, D.C.

☐ CHECK HERE IF YOU WOULD LIKE TO HAVE A DIFFERENT **DINING IN**— COOKBOOK SENT TO YOU ONCE A MONTH

Payable by Mastercard, Visa or C.O.D. Returnable if not satisfied.
$7.95 plus $1.00 postage and handling for each book.

BILL TO: SHIP TO:

Name _____   Name _____

Address _____   Address _____

City _____ State _____ Zip _____   City _____ State _____ Zip _____

☐ Payment enclosed   ☐ Send COD

☐ Charge   Name _____

Visa # _____   Address _____

Exp. Date _____   City _____ State _____ Zip _____

Mastercard # _____

Exp. Date _____

                 Name _____

                 Address _____

Signature _____   City _____ State _____ Zip _____

PEANUT BUTTER PUBLISHING

PEANUT BUTTER TOWERS • 2733 - 4TH AVENUE SOUTH • SEATTLE, WA 98134